ESSAYS IN
IDLENESS

YOSHIDA KENKŌ

TRANSLATED BY G.B. SANSOM

COSIMO CLASSICS

NEW YORK

Essays in Idleness
© 2005 Cosimo, Inc.

Cosimo, P.O. Box 416
Old Chelsea Station
New York, NY 10113-0416

or visit our website at:
www.cosimobooks.com

Essays in Idleness originally published in 1911.

Library of Congress Cataloging-in-Publication Data
A catalog record for this book is available from the Library of Congress

Cover design by www.wiselephant.com

ISBN: 1-59605-062-4

The Tsurezure Gusa of Yoshida Kenkō

To while away the idle hours, seated the livelong day before the ink-slab, by jotting down without order or purpose whatever trifling thoughts pass through my mind, verily this is a queer and crazy thing to do!

1. Lo! To those that are born into this world many indeed are the desirable things.

Exceedingly worshipful is the majesty of the emperor. The youngest leaves of the bamboo garden* are not of the seed of men, and such as they are out of reach of all human desires. Lofty the estate of the prime minister beyond all dispute, and those of such station as to have a retinue from the court are of great splendour, while their children and their grandchildren, though their fortunes be decayed, still preserve some of the grandeur of their forbears.

But in all ranks of life beneath these, though a man may rise and prosper and show a boastful front, nevertheless, fine as he may think himself, it is forsooth but a sorry thing he has achieved.

No lot is so little envied as a priest's. Sei Shōnagon wrote, 'They are looked upon as so many bits of stick', and truly this is so. Nor is a priest admired who is forceful and turbulent, for men feel, in the words of the sage Zōga, that thirst for fame means disregard of Buddha's law.

There is indeed none but the complete hermit who leads a desirable life.

What men chiefly covet is outward excellence, of figure and of

---

* i.e. descendants of the imperial family.

bearing. They seek and are not wearied by the company of one who has a pleasing manner of speech, talking with charm but not garrulity. Yet how it pains one to see revealed in a man a base nature that belies a fair exterior. Beauty and rank, indeed, are such as we are born with: but, for the mind – if a man strive to copy the sages, shall he not succeed and grow from wisdom unto greater wisdom? And if he lacks wisdom, then, though his form be fair and his heart good, he feels outshone and ill at ease in the company of others, even of low degree and unpleasing aspect.

It is desirable to have a knowledge of true literature, of composition and versifying, of wind and string instruments; and it is well, moreover, to be learned in precedent and court ceremonies, so as to be a model for others. One should write not unskilfully in the running hand, be able to sing in a pleasing voice and keep good time to music; and, lastly, a man should not refuse a little wine when pressed upon him.

2. Wanton and heedless must one hold those who, forgetting this benevolent rule of the great ones of old, reckless of the people's sorrow and the country's harm, delight to exhaust all forms of luxury, and live withal cramped by their own magnificence. In Lord Kujō's admonitions to his descendants it is written, 'From your headdress and your garments to your horse and your carriage, be content with what you have, and do not seek for elegance and splendour.' So, in his august writings on palace affairs, Emperor Juntoku says, 'In all things for the emperor's use plainness is desirable.'

3. However gifted and accomplished a young man may be, if he has no fondness for women, one has a feeling of something lacking, as of a precious winecup without a bottom. Admire the condition of a lover! Drenched with dews and frosts and aimlessly wandering, ever concerned to shun the world's reproof and escape his parents' reproaches, hither and thither pursued by doubt and distress – and spending his nights withal sleepless upon a solitary couch.

But it is well that a man do not become addicted to lewdness, a constant and familiar companion of women.

4. Happy is the man who, mindful of the after life, is diligent in the way of Buddha.

5. Not he who, plunged in grief at his misfortunes, takes the tonsure because he holds the world harsh and evil, but rather he who shuts himself off completely and lives day in, day out, expecting nothing, demanding nothing – this is the true hermit.

Well may one feel, as the Chūnagon Akimoto said, 'O! To look on the moon guiltless in exile.'

6. Even for the great, to say nothing of the lowly, it is well to be childless. The prince imperial first minister of the middle Kaneakira, the prime minister Kujō and the minister of the left Hanazono all held it a good thing to be without posterity. Well was it too that the minister of Somedono was without offspring; and it is written in the *Yotsugi no okina no monogatari* that it is an evil thing when a man's descendants fall behind him. Indeed, it is related that Prince Shō toku, when he caused his own tomb to be built, cut off and stopped up the paths thereto, because he meant to leave no offspring.

7. Were we to live on for ever – were the dews of Adashino never to vanish, the smoke on Toribeyama never to fade away – then indeed would men not feel the pity of things.

Truly the beauty of life is its uncertainty. Of all living things, none lives so long as man. Consider how the ephemera* awaits the fall of evening, and the summer cicada knows neither spring nor autumn. Even a year of life lived peacefully seems long and happy beyond compare; but for such as never weary of this world and are loth to die, a thousand years would pass away like the dream of a single night.

What shall it avail a man to drag out till he becomes decrepit and unsightly a life which some day needs must end. Long life brings many shames. At most before his fortieth year is full it is seemly for a man to die.

After that age it is pitiful to see how, unashamed of his looks, he loves to thrust himself into the society of others, and cherishing his offspring in the evening of his days, craves to live

* The mayfly.

on and on that he may watch them grow and prosper. So he continues, his heart set on naught but worldliness, and hardening to the pity of things.

8. Of all things that lead astray the heart of man there is naught like fleshly lust. What a weakly thing is this heart of ours. Though a perfume, for example, is but a transient thing, and though he knows full well that incense is burned to give an odour to garments, yet a man's heart will always be stirred by a vague perfume.

The magician of Kume, the legend runs, lost his magic power through looking at the white shins of a maiden washing clothes. This may well have been, for here was no charm from without, but the real beauty of plump and glistening limbs.

9. What strikes man most in a woman is the beauty of her hair, and from her manner of speech you may tell her quality and her disposition, though she be hidden from view.

Even to look on her as she goes about her business will sometimes lead the heart astray – for she will sleep in uneasy postures, spare no bodily pain and bear with patience unbearable discomforts, all because her mind is set on love.

Verily the roots of passion are deep, and remote its sources. Though the lusts and appetites of the six defilers* are many, yet may they all be banished save this one alone. It can hardly be uprooted, and young and old, wise and foolish are alike its slaves.

Therefore it is said that with a rope in which are twisted strands of a woman's hair the mighty elephant may be bound, and that the deer in autumn will not fail to gather to the call of a pipe carved from the clogs a woman wears.

It is this madness which we must chastise in ourselves, which we must dread and which we must guard against.

10. There is a charm about a neat and proper dwelling house, although this world, 'tis true, is but a temporary abode. Even the moonshine seems to gain in friendly brilliancy, striking into the house where a good man lives in peaceful ease.

---

* The mind and the senses.

The man is to be envied who lives in a house, not of the modern, garish kind, but set among venerable trees, with a garden where plants grow wild and yet seem to have been disposed with care, verandas and fences tastefully arranged, and all its furnishings simple but antique.

A house which multitudes of workmen have devoted all their ingenuity to decorate, where rare and strange things from home and abroad are set out in array, and where even the trees and shrubs are trained unnaturally – such is an unpleasant sight, depressing to look at, to say nothing of spending one's days therein. Nor, gazing on it, can one but reflect how easily it might vanish in a moment of time.

The appearance of a house is in some sort an index to the character of its occupant.

There is a story that Saigyō, when he saw that the minister Gotokudaiji had stretched ropes across the roof of his residence in order to keep the kites from settling there, exclaimed, 'And if the kites do settle there, what harm can they do? This then is the sort of man his Lordship is!' And ever after refused to visit him.

So, when I once saw ropes stretched on the palace roof of his Highness Prince Ayanokōji, I remembered this story, but then I heard people say that the truth was, his Highness could not bear to see the frogs in his pond caught by crows that settled there in flocks, and I thought this is a very praiseworthy action; and, after all, we cannot tell but what Gotokudaiji had some good reason for what he did.

11. Once in the month of September I passed over the plain of Kurusu and sought out a certain village among the hills beyond, when, threading my way far down a narrow moss-grown path, I came upon a lonely hut. There was never a sound to greet me, save the dripping of water from a pipe buried in fallen leaves, but I knew that someone lived there, for sprays of chrysanthemum and maple leaves bestrewed the shelf before the shrine, and 'Ah!' thought I, 'in such a place a man can spend his days.' But as I stood and gazed in wonder, I perceived in the garden beyond a great orange tree, its branches weighed down with fruit. It was strongly closed in on all sides by a fence. This broke the spell, and I thought to myself, 'If only yonder tree had not been there!'

12. It would be a joyful thing indeed to hold intimate converse with a man after one's own heart, chatting without reserve about things of interest or the fleeting topics of the world; but such, alas, are few and far between. Not that one desires a companion who will sit opposite and never utter a word in contradiction – one might as well be alone. Far better in hours of loneliness the company of one who, while he will listen with respect to your views, will disagree a little and argue, saying 'Yes, that is so, but . . . ' or 'For this reason such and such is the case.'

And yet, with those who are not of the same way of thinking or are contentious, a man can only discuss things of passing interest, for the truth is, there must not be any wide gulf between real bosom friends.

13. To sit alone in the lamplight with a book spread out before you, and hold intimate converse with men of unseen generations – such is a pleasure beyond compare.

Of such books there are the wonderful volumes of *Wen Hsüan*, the works of Po Chü-i, the sayings of Lao-tzu and the *Chuang-tzu*; while there are many admirable things written in olden times by scholars of our own land.

14. Then, too, there is a charm in our native poetry. Described in verse, the rude toil of the lowly peasant of the hills becomes pleasing, and even the dreadful wild boar, in such phrases as 'lair of the couchant boar', sounds gentle.

As for the verses of today, though there is an occasional line which seems apt and graceful, there are none which conjure up a moving picture, beyond the mere words, as in the old poems. Tsurayuki's poem beginning 'Our ways are not like threads'* was looked upon, tradition says, as the rubbish of the *Kokinshū*, and yet there is not a man living who can write such verse nowadays. Why this one poem was picked out for blame it is hard to tell, seeing that there are numbers of poems from that

---

* 'Our ways are not like threads, that can be twisted into a single strand, but are separate, wherefore we feel "thin-hearted" [forlorn].'

period similar in form and expression. In the *Genji Monogatari* the line is written slightly differently. The same is said of the poem 'Even the remaining pines are lonely on the peak' occurring in the *Shinkokinshū*, and it certainly does seem a little clumsy. Yet in Ienaga's diary, it is stated that the committee of judges reported favourably on this poem, and that his Majesty afterwards was greatly pleased with it.

Although it is generally said that the art of poetry is the one thing that has never changed since olden times, yet, with the same themes and words as are in use today, look how different are the verses composed by the ancients. What *they* wrote was simple and artless, pure in form and full of feeling.

Many indeed are the beautiful passages in songs and poems from the anthology called *Ryōjin Hishō*. Somehow there is always a charm about even the most impromptu and careless sayings of the men of bygone days.

15. It wakes one up to go away from home for a time, no matter whither. Rambling and exploring about the countryside you come upon a host of unwonted sights in rustic spots and mountain hamlets. You get a messenger to take letters to the capital, and you write and say do not forget to send me so and so by the next opportunity. All this is in its way amusing. Of course you have a thousand things to think of in such a place.

Pleasant also to slip away and go into retreat in some mountain temple.

16. Shut up in seclusion in a mountain temple, devoting oneself to the service of Buddha, one is never lonely, and feels one's heart cleansed of its impurity.

17. It is well for a man to be frugal, to abstain from luxury, to possess no treasure nor to covet this world's goods. Since olden times there has rarely been a sage who was wealthy.

In China there was once a man called Hsü Yü. He had not a single possession in the world, and even scooped up water with his hands, until a friend gave him a gourd. But one day, when he had hung it from a branch, it rattled in the wind; whereupon, disturbed by the noise, he threw it away and once more took to drinking from out of his clasped hands. How pure and free the heart of such a man.

18. Sun Ch'en spent the winter months without bedclothes. He had one bundle of straw, which he slept on at night and put away in the daytime.

The Chinese, admiring these things exceedingly, have set them down in their writings so that they might be handed on to future generations. Our people do not even pass [such stories] on by word of mouth.

19. The changes of the seasons are powerful to make men feel all around them the wonder of things, and, people say, the autumn most of all. Not without truth, indeed, but even more meseems does the look of spring make a man's bosom swell. The song of the birds is full of a springlike sound, and under the warm sunshine the grasses of the hedgerows burst into bud. So the spring deepens and the hazes spread abroad, and then the flowers at last begin to blossom – when lo, the wind blows and the rain falls incessantly, and they are scattered in dismay. So everything is grief until at length the green leaves come.

More even than the orange blossom, famed though it be, does the scent of the plum make one recall the past with longing. So the bright kerria and the soft-hued wisteria arouse a crowd of feelings that cannot be dismissed.

About the time of the Washing of Buddha and the Kamo festival, when the young leaves grow thickly on the tree-tops – then too, someone has said with truth, the sadness of life and the longing for lost friends are at their height. In the fifth month, when iris leaves are scattered on the roofs and the young rice planted out, the cry of the waterfowl is full of melancholy.

Then in the sixth month the white evening-glory and the smoke of the herbs burned to drive off mosquitoes, rising from some lowly cottage, make a touching sight. An imposing ceremony, too, is the purification of the sixth month.

The feast of Tanabata is bright and gay. Now, as the nights grow cooler, the wild geese come crying, the leaves of the lespedeza start to redden, the rice of the first crop is reaped and dried. No season is so crowded with events as autumn.

Fine, too, the scene after an autumn gale has blown.

Here as I string these thoughts together I must perforce repeat the old familiar sayings of the *Genji Monogatari*, the *Pillow Book* and suchlike works; nor am I indeed loth to say the same things over again. I have let my pen run on aimlessly, because a man is ill at ease if he does not say the things he feels, and, after all, this is only to be thrown away and not to be seen by others.

Now come the scenes of winter decay, little inferior to those of autumn. The reddened leaves fall and settle among the grasses by the water's edge, and on a morning white with frost the vapour rises from the water pipes. There is no time like that when the year is drawing to a close, and everyone rushes busily to and fro. After the twentieth day the aspect of the sky is melancholy – dreary with the clear cold moon that none will gaze upon. Solemn and grand the celebration of the Ritual of the Names of the Buddha, and the departure of the envoys to the imperial tombs. The palace is busy with ceremonies and preparations for the coming spring.

Then comes the Expulsion of Demons, followed closely by the Adoration of the Four Quarters in an interesting way.

In the thick darkness of the last night of the year the people run about with pine-wood flares, knocking at folks' doors till past the middle of the night, shouting (I do not know why) noisily, and flying hither and thither. But as the day dawns even they become quiet, and sadly we take our leave of the departing year.

It is a pity that the custom of worshipping the spirits of the dead, who were said to return on that night, is no longer observed in the capital, though in the east it is still practised.

So with the dawn of the New Year, though the sky wears the same look as yesterday, by contrast one feels as if some change had taken place. Pine trees set out along the broad streets give a bright and cheerful aspect – another moving sight.

20. A certain recluse, I know not who, once said that no bonds attached him to this life, and the only thing he would regret to leave behind was the sky. Truly one feels this to be so.

21. At all times it is a soothing thing to gaze upon the moon. That was a pretty dispute where, one saying that there was nothing so delightful as the moon, another replied that he considered the dew a more moving sight. But indeed, in its due season, what is there that does not rouse the emotions? The moon and blossoms go without saying; but even the wind alone is noticed. A clear stream breaking upon rocks makes a delightful picture, whatever the season.

Is it not a touching verse of the Chinese poet which says:

> The streams called Yüan and Hsiang
> Flow eastward day and night,
> And never cease – heedless of the grief of man.

Hsi K'ang said that it was his heart's delight to sport among the hills and streams and gaze at birds and fishes. There is no such quiet bliss as to wander in secluded spots where grass is green and water clear.

22. In all things one looks back with regret to the past. Modern fashions appear to be growing from bad to worse. It is the ancient shapes that are most pleasing in the beautiful utensils made by workers in wood. As for the style of letters, even a scrap of waste paper from olden times is admirable.

Everyday speech, too, is growing regrettably bad. Whereas they used to say 'Lift up the carriage' and 'Turn up the lamps', now they have changed the way they prononce it. Old people say that it is a great pity that for the assembly of servants of the Household Department they now say 'Get up and light the lamps', and at the recital of the *Golden Light Sutra*, instead of saying 'Hall of the Imperial Lecture' they say 'Lecture Hall'.

23. But despite the degeneracy of these latter days, happily the nine-times-encircled imperial palace still remains aloof from the world, serene and venerable as of yore. Fine-sounding names are used, such as the Platform of the Dews, the Dry Rice of the Morning and the divers styles of gates and halls. Even the names of such things as are in the houses of the common people, blinds, verandas and doors, are pleasing to the ear.

I like to hear the command 'Make ready for the night' in the nobles' quarters, and the cry 'Hasten to light the lamps in his Majesty's Bedchamber', or to see the great ministers performing their offices. It is amusing to watch the important air of the high officials' underlings, or to see them on a coldish night dozing as they sit here and there the whole night through.

The prime minister Tokudaiji said, 'I love to hear the beautiful sound of the bell in the Shrine of the Sacred Mirror.'

24. I know of nothing more touching and interesting than the departure of the vestal princess for the Shrine on the Moor.

Another interesting thing is the way in which the words 'prayer' and 'buddha' are considered unpropitious, and in their stead are used 'coloured paper' and 'child of the centre'.

Splendid and unforgettable are the shrines of the gods. How fine they look in their groves of ancient trees that wear an unworldly air, set round with the jewel-fence and on the sacred *saka* tree the white cloth symbols hung.

First among them are the shrines of Ise, Kamo, Kasuga, Hirano, Sumiyoshi, Miwa, Kibune, Yoshida, Ōharano, Matsuo and Amenomiya.

25. The pools and shallows of the river Asuka! This is all in-constant life. Time passes, things vanish. Joy and grief go and come. What once was a gay and crowded spot becomes a deserted moor, or, if the dwelling rests unchanged, yet those within are not the same. 'The peach and the pear tree cannot speak. With whom then shall I talk of bygone days?' How much more fleeting, then, the traces of the great that lived in ages we have never seen.

Looking on the homes built long ago by the regent Fujiwara Michinaga, the Kyōgokuden or the Hōjōji, one stands amazed to see how a man's ambition can come to nought, and to note the changes wrought by time.

When Michinaga built and decorated his palace and greatly added to his lands, hoping to make his descendants guardians of the throne and protectors of the people, little can he have thought that in any times such desolation would overtake them. The Great Gate and the Golden Pavilion remained until a little while ago, but the South Gate was burned in Shōwa [1312-16] while the Golden Pavilion collapsed soon afterwards, and left untouched, has never been set up again. Only the Hall of Everlasting Life remains in its former shape. The nine great Buddhas stand in a stately row, and one can still see plainly a tablet written by Counsellor Gyōzei and doors painted by Kaneyuki – a moving sight.

The Hokkedō still remains, but for how long? Others there are, less well-remembered spots, where but the stone foundations now are left, though no one knows for certain what building once stood there.

Therefore it is vain in all things for a man to set his thoughts on a time he will not live to see.

26. Though the breeze blow not, the flower of the heart of man will change its hue. Now looking back on months and years of intimacy, to feel your friend, while you still remember the moving words you exchanged, yet growing distant and living in a world apart – all this is sadder far than partings brought by death.

It is the old lament – that the white thread must be dyed, and the ways part at the crossroads.

In the *Hundred Poems of the Emperor Horikawa* there is one which reads:

> Below the fence which erstwhile stood
> Around my loved one's bower
> Now only grow the violet,
> The wild tsubana flower.

Truly a melancholy scene.

27. At the ceremony of abdication the handing over of the Sword, the Jewel and the Mirror is an occasion beyond measure melancholy.

When the late emperor Hanazono descended from the throne he is said to have composed this verse:

> Deserted by the Palace serving-men
> My unswept garden's thick with fallen flowers,

meaning to say that, busy with the affairs of the new sovereign, they left him neglected in his retirement.

Such occasions reveal the true character of those about one.

28. The year of mourning for the death of an emperor is surely a time of unequalled sadness.

The house of mourning is a melancholy sight, with low planked floor, hung with blinds woven from reeds and bordered with coarse linen, and supplied with the roughest of furnishings, while all about wear unwonted garments, even to their swords and the loops of their girdles.

29. In hours of quiet thought one cannot but be overcome by longing for the past.

When, to while away the long nights after folk have gone to rest, we go through our odd belongings, sometimes, as we throw away such scraps of paper as we do not want to keep, the handwriting of one who is no more, or an idle sketch maybe, will catch the eye and vividly recall the moment it was made.

It is affecting, too, after the lapse of many years, to come across the letters even of one who is still living, and to call to mind the year and the occasion when they were written.

The things they were wont to use — they have no heart, but they remain unchanged throughout the long, long years. A melancholy reflection.

30. There is no such mournful time as follows on a death. For the days of retirement a crowd of people go up together to some mountain village, into a cramped and incommodious house, and there they busily perform the offices for the dead. So the appointed time passes with unwonted quickness. The last day is pitiless indeed; for in silence they gather together their possessions, each for himself, and go their several ways. Only when they have returned to their own homes will they begin to feel exceeding sad.

Months and years pass by, and still they do not forget, though, as the saying goes, the departed grows more distant every day. However that may be, they seem not to feel so deeply as at the time of death, for now they chatter and laugh together. The body is laid to rest upon some lonely mountain side, whither the mourners come on rare appointed days; soon the tablet is overgrown with moss, buried in fallen leaves, and looks in time as if none came to visit there save even storms and the nocturnal moon.

There may be some who will recall the dead, and think of him with grief. But soon they themselves must pass away. Then how can later generations grieve, who only know him by repute? After a time they go no longer to his tomb, and the people do not even know his name or who he was. True, some feeling folk may gaze with pity on what is now but the growth of grasses of succeeding springs; but at last there comes a day when even the pine trees that groaned in the storms, not lasting out their thousand years of life, are split for fuel, and the ancient grave, dug up and turned to rice-field, leaves never a trace behind.

31. One morning, after a fine fall of snow, I had to write to a friend, but in my letter I said not a word about the snow. Whereupon the answer came, 'How can I do what is asked of me by a man of such poor taste as not to write "What do you think of this snowfall" or a line of that sort? Really I am ashamed of you.' I thought this an amusing reply. The writer is now dead, so that I do not readily forget even such a trifle as this.

32. Once, about the 20th day of the ninth month, a friend invited me to stroll about with him till daybreak looking at the moon. As we walked, he bethought himself of a friend's house, where he called and was conducted within. There was something impressive in the sequestered air of this desolate garden, wet with dew, where breathed a faint natural perfume. Betimes my friend came out, but I, still feeling the strange beauty of the scene, stood for a while hidden in the shade, and so perceived his host, instead of forthwith hastening to retire, open the shutters a little wider, as if to gaze upon the moon; and as he could not have known that he was being watched, it must have been because he was at all times fond of such things. I heard that he soon after passed away.

33. When the present palace was completed, it was inspected by those versed in ancient customs and they had no fault to find. The day for his Majesty's removal to the new Palace was drawing near, when Princess Genki very admirably pointed out that the comb-shaped openings in the wall of the old Kan'in-den were round, and without edging. The fact being that it was a mistake to have made them foliated and edged with wood, they were therefore altered.

35. Even if your handwriting is bad, it is well to write your own letters unashamed. To have them written by others because your own hand is unsightly is a nuisance.

36. It is a great relief and very pleasant, when you have neglected to write for a long time – and thinking 'How angry she must be with me', you feel conscious of your guilt and do not know how to approach her – to get a message from a woman, saying, 'I want a manservant. Can you spare me one?' Such a disposition is very admirable, so people say – and with reason.

37. Although some will say, 'After all this time, why stand on ceremony?' I myself feel that it is a sign of genuine and proper feeling when even the most inseparable friends treat each another, if the occasion demands, with due reserve and decorum. On the other hand, it is sometimes well for people who are not intimate to speak freely.

38. Enslaved by desire for name and profit, to live a life tortured by care, with never a moment's peace, is foolish indeed. Such as are rich in treasure are poor in virtue. By its means men purchase evil and invite disaster. When they are dead, though they have piled their gold up to the constellation of the Bear, they do but bring distress on others. It is a poor thing to take delight in gladdening the eyes of fools. Great carriages, sleek horses, ornaments of gold and jewels – all these a man of understanding looks upon as folly. Throw your gold away among the mountains. Cast into the stream your jewels. Exceedingly foolish are men whom greed for profit leads astray.

It seems a desirable thing to leave for long years behind one an unburied name. But a man is not perforce superior because he is of noble family or high degree. Foolish and unskilful people, thanks to birth or opportunity, sometimes rise to high rank and live in great state, while saints and sages, lacking opportunity, have lived and died in humble stations.

Only less foolish therefore is the desire for rank and office.

If we reflect on the desire to leave behind a name for excellence of heart and head, we see that the love of fame is a delight in the approval of others. But neither those who praise nor those who blame remain long of this world, and those to whom they tell the tale must presently depart. Whose praise do you covet? Whose blame do you dread? Praise is the fountain of blame. Though your fame live on, it profits nothing, and this desire comes next in foolishness.

Speaking of such as persist in the mere search for skill and wisdom, it must be said that with the growth of knowledge comes falsehood; increasing talent brings increasing care.

True knowledge is not gained by precept or by study. What then is knowledge? Right and wrong are one. What is good and what evil? The true man has neither knowledge nor virtue. He is without deeds, without name. Who then shall know him, who shall speak his fame? Not that he conceals his virtue, nor cherishes his unwisdom, but because he is beyond the confines of wisdom and of ignorance, of gain and of loss.

So much for those that set their deluded hearts on fame and profit. All things are nothing – unworthy of speech, unworthy of desire.

39. The reverend priest Hōnen, when asked by a man who said he was overcome with drowsiness while at his prayers and so neglected his religious duties, what he ought to do to rid himself of this hindrance, replied, 'Pray earnestly enough to keep awake.'

Another admirable saying of his was 'If you think your salvation assured, it is assured. If you think it is not assured, it is not assured,' And another, 'If, while you doubt, you notwithstanding pray, even then you will be saved.'

40. In the province of Inaba there was a girl, the daughter of a certain lay priest of noble family, whose hand was asked in marriage by many that heard of her beauty. However this girl ate nothing but chestnuts, never touching rice or other grain, and her parents therefore refused, saying that such an unusual thing ought not to be seen by others.

41. Once at the horse-races during the Kamo festival on the 5th of the fifth month, unable to see for the crowd between us and our carriage, we all got down and made towards the railings, but the press of people standing was too great, and we could not push our way through. Just at this time we saw a priest who had climbed up a tree over against us, and was seated in a fork to get a view. As he clung to his perch, time after time he dozed off, and only awoke when on the point of falling. The spectators jeered and reviled him, saying, 'What a fool the fellow is calmly to fall asleep up there in such a risky place!'

When I heard this I was struck with a thought, and exclaimed, 'And what of us, who spend the days in sightseeing, forgetting that death may come at any moment? We are greater fools than he!' Whereupon those in front turned round, remarking, 'That is indeed so. It is exceedingly foolish', and making way for us, they invited us to pass forward, saying, 'Come this way, sirs.'

Though this remark of mine might have occurred to anybody, I suppose it was because it came as a surprise to them at the moment that they were so impressed. Men are not sticks and stones, and a word in season will sometimes affect them.

42. There was once a priest, son of one Karahashi Chūjō, who was called the Bishop Gyōga, and was an instructor of novices studying the doctrines of his sect. He suffered from a rising of vapours to the head, which grew worse year by year until his nostrils were stopped up and he had difficulty in breathing. They tried all sorts of remedies but his sufferings only increased, and his eyes, eyebrows and forehead became one swollen mass, overhanging so that he could not see. He was a horrible sight, and looked like the grotesque mask used for the ni-no-mai dance. So his face grew like a demon's, his eyes high up on his head, his

nose spread all over his face, until at last he shut himself up, and even the people belonging to the temple could not see him.

So he continued for many years, still growing worse and worse, until at last he died. To think that there are such sicknesses in the world!

43. One day towards the close of spring in calm and lovely weather, I came upon a seemly house, in a garden stretching far back, grown with venerable trees and strewn with faded blossoms. I could not pass without a look, and peeping in, I saw that all the shutters on the southern side were down, giving the place a deserted air; but facing east the doors were thrown open, and through a rent in the blind I saw a handsome young man of about twenty, who though quite at his ease, was sitting there dignified and calm, reading a volume spread out before him on the desk.

I felt a great desire to find out who and what manner of man he was.

44. Once I saw emerging from within a coarse, bamboo-plaited gate a very young man, of important mien, wearing a rich silken hunting-robe, whose hue the moon obscured, but which was embroidered in deep colours. Attended by one small boy, he took the path stretching far away among rice fields, brushing through the young plants wet with dew, and playing to himself the while with unspeakable sweetness on a flute. As he went on – little thinking that there was one who listened with admiration – curious to see where he was going I followed him with my eyes until he ceased to play, and went in at a temple gate by the foot of the hill.

A carriage propped up on its shafts attracts more attention here in the country than in the capital. I enquire of my servants and they reply, 'Such and such a prince is now here. It is no doubt some Buddhist rite they are performing.' Priests and others are assembled in the hall, and on the cool evening breeze comes a pervading odour of incense. The way in which the maids of honour take care their garments shall not flutter in the breeze they make as they pass along the gallery to the royal apartments shows that they are careful to preserve decorum even here in this hillside village where none can see them.

Here the autumn moor, in wanton luxuriant growth, is flooded with the heavy fall of dew; insects sing noisily; and the water in the pipes flows with a soothing sound. The clouds seem to gather and disperse more rapidly than in the sky of the capital, the moon to wear a more variable complexion.

45. The elder brother of Prince Kin'yo was the bishop Ryōgaku, a mighty choleric man. Near his house in the temple grounds there was a large celtis-tree (*enoki*), so that he was known as the Celtis Tree Bishop. Disliking this, he had the tree cut down, but as the roots remained, people now called him the Tree Stump Bishop. At last, highly incensed, he had the stump dug up and thrown away, leaving a large hole behind. Whereat they now named him the Hole-in-the Ground Bishop.

46. Near Yanagiwara there was a priest known as His Reverence Robbery-by-Violence. This name was given to him because he had several times been the victim of robbers.

47. A certain man, on a pilgrimage to Kiyomizu, joined on the way an old nun. As they went on their journey, she kept on saying *Kushame, kushame*, and he asked her, 'Pray, what is that you are saying? But she made no answer, and continued to repeat those words. At last, when he had asked her several times, her patience gave out, and she said, 'They say that when you sneeze you will die unless this spell is repeated, and I am repeating it now because my young master, who is at Mount Hiei, may be sneezing at this moment.' Indeed a faithful heart!

48. When Lord Mitsuchika was performing the duties of officer of the lectures on the *Golden Light Sutra* to the retired emperor, his Majesty summoned him to the presence and caused food to be served to him. When he had eaten he took the trays with the leavings, pushed them under the screen, and departed. The waiting-women cried out 'Ah! How nasty! Whom does he expect to take this?' But his Majesty was much impressed, and said that this conduct of one versed in ancient customs was admirable.

49. Beware of putting off the practice of religion until your old age. The ancient tombs are mostly those of such as died in their youth.

Only when suddenly stricken down by illness, and on the point of death, do men first recognize the errors of their past life. And what are these errors? Nought but delaying those things which should be done quickly, and hastening those things which should be delayed; whereby is caused great regret for the past. When his time comes, what shall it avail a man then to repent?

Our hearts should be firmly fixed on the imminence of death, which we ought never for a moment to forget. So shall we be little soiled by the contamination of this world, and our hearts earnest in the observance of the way of Buddha.

One of the saints of old, according to Zenrin's *Ten Karmic Causes*, when folk came to talk on business, used to say to them, 'I have a pressing task before me. My time is close at hand.' And shutting his ears, would continue his prayers. So he went on until he one day passed away.

Another sage named Shinkai was so impressed by the fleeting nature of this life that he never even sat at his ease, but always remained squatting.

50. In the period of Ōchō [1311-12] a story got about that there had been brought up to the capital from Ise a woman who had turned into a demon. At that time the people of the city and suburbs used to go out in crowds every day, 'to see the demon'. 'Yesterday she was at Saionji's,' the rumour would be. 'Today she is going to be taken to the emperor', or 'Now she is at such and such a place', but nobody could say he had really seen her. All ranks and conditions talked of nothing but this demon. One day, at this time, when I was going from Higashiyama towards Agui, I met a great crowd of people from Shijō and above, all rushing northwards and shouting, 'The demon is at Muromachi, in Ichijō.' Looking from the Imadegawa side I saw that they were packed about the emperor's staging so close that there was no chance of passing through, and thinking that there could hardly be such a to-do without some reason I sent to enquire, but no one could be found that had met her. They stood there, a shouting mob, until dusk, when they began to brawl and quarrel.

It happened at this time that many people were taken with sickness for two or three days; and some said, of the false rumour of the demon, that it was an omen thereof!

51. When the emperor desired to bring water from the River Ōi to his residence at Kameyama he had a waterwheel made by the villagers of Ōi. At great expense and after several days they at last managed to finish it, but it would hardly go round at all. They tried to put it right in all sorts of ways, but without success – it would not revolve, and they had set it up in vain.

Finally they called the villagers of Uji, and had them make a wheel. This they built with ease. It went round properly and took up the water in a most satisfactory way.

In all things there is nothing like one who knows his business thoroughly.

52. In the Ninnaji there was a priest who, to his great regret, had reached old age without ever making a pilgrimage to Iwashimizu.* So one day he made up his mind and set off alone on foot. He worshipped at the Gokurakuji and at the Kōra shrines [at the bottom of the hill] and then, thinking this was all, returned home. There he related how he had accomplished the desire of many years, and found the shrines even more sublime than he had heard. 'But,' he said, 'I wonder why everybody who came to worship went up the hill? Though it was very beautiful, my purpose was to worship the gods, so I did not go to see the hill.'

A guide is desirable, even in small matters.

53. This is another story, of the priests of the Ninnaji. They had a feast to celebrate the farewell to the world of a young acolyte about to enter the priesthood. In their revels they became drunken, and the acolyte, beginning to feel merry, took a three-legged iron pot that lay near by, and put it on his head. Then, though it fitted very tight, he flattened out his nose, pulled the pot over his face and began to dance. The whole company grew merry beyond measure, until after performing awhile, he at

---

* At the summit of which hill was a shrine to the deity Hachiman.

length tried to pull it off – but in vain! This sobered the feast, and they were thrown into confusion and doubt, wondering what they should do. While they were debating it cut into his head, and blood began to flow and his face swelled up so that he could hardly breathe. They tried to break it, but it was not easily broken, and as the force of the blow went to his head, he could not bear it, and they were obliged to stop. They did not know what to do next, so throwing over the three legs, which looked like horns, a black gauze cloak, they led him, supported by a staff, to the house of a physician in Kyōto. People looked at them with amazement as they went along. It must have been a queer scene when they brought him face to face with the physician on entering his house. When he spoke, his voice was muffled, and resounded so that they could not hear what he said. The physician said that he had never seen such a case in the books, nor had he ever had any oral instruction on the point, so they were obliged to return to the temple. There, his friends and relatives, with his old mother, gathered at his bedside and wept and grieved – not that they thought he could hear! At last someone said, 'Suppose he does lose his ears and nose, so far as living goes there is no reason why he should not survive. Let us then pull the thing off by main force.' So they thrust rice straw all round between his head and the metal, and pulled as if to drag off his head. His ears and nose were torn away, and he escaped with his bare life, suffering afterwards for many a long day.

54. In the same temple there was a beautiful young acolyte whom certain of the priests planned to invite with them on an excursion. Some of the performing priests put their heads together, and carefully prepared a packet of refreshments, which they placed in a sort of box and carried to a suitable spot on Narabi-no-oka, where they buried it, covering the place with fallen leaves, so as to hide any unusual appearance; and then, returning to the temple, asked him to accompany them.

In joyful mood they roamed around, disporting themselves, until at last, thoroughly exhausted, they sat down in a ring on the soft carpet of moss that lay at their feet.

Here they all cried 'If someone would but burn the reddened leaves' [ie. to warm some sake]. 'Let those priests whose prayers are efficacious see what they can do.' Thereupon they turned to the tree at the foot of which the things were buried, rattled their heads, made tremendous invocations, and altogether a great to-do. Then they scraped away the leaves, and lo – there was nothing, not a thing, to be seen. Thinking they might have mistaken the place, they ranged all over the hill side, digging everywhere, but without success. Someone must have seen them burying something, and stolen it while they were gone to the temple. Crestfallen and ashamed, the priests began to wrangle in an unseemly manner, and returned home in great wrath.

Things which we look forward to enjoying with great zest are certain to end in disappointment.

55. A house should be built with the summer in view. In winter one can live anywhere, but a poor dwelling in summer is unbearable. Deep water does not give a cool sensation. Far cooler is a shallow running stream. Coming to details, a room with sliding doors is lighter than one with those on hinges. When the ceiling is high the room is cold in winter and difficult to light. In construction people agree in admiring a place with plenty of spare room, as being pleasing to the eye and at the same time useful for all sorts of purposes.

56. How lacking in taste is it for people who meet you at rare intervals to talk on and on, relating all that has happened to themselves in the meantime. Why, even one's close and intimate friends are diffident at the first meeting after a lengthy separation!

People of the lower orders, even among strangers, delight in breathlessly recounting something which they consider interesting; while the well-bred man, though in a large gathering, will address his conversation to one person only, and others will listen of their own accord.

Common people entering a large company address themselves to no one in particular, relating incidents as if they had just seen them, and every one bursts into noisy laughter – very loud and vulgar.

One can judge of a man's breeding by seeing whether he refrains from excessive mirth on hearing a funny remark, or on the other hand laughs loudly at something which is not amusing.

It is an unpleasant thing to hear a man, when the appearance of others is being discussed, or when someone says, 'Intelligent people do so and so', put *himself* forward as a standard of comparison.

57. People make a great mistake when in talking of poetry they quote with approval bad verses. If they had a little knowledge of the art they would not praise them. In all things it is ludicrous and annoying to hear a man discourse upon a subject with which he is not in the least acquainted.

58. Those who say 'If a man be religious at heart, it matters not where he dwells. There is nothing to prevent him from looking forward to the future life, even though he remain at home and mix with his fellows' – such people do not at all understand what future life means.

How can anyone, forsooth, who feels the vanity of this world, and desires to pass beyond the confines of life and death, earnestly devote himself day and night to the service of his lord and the care of his house?

Since a man's heart is moved and changed by worldly ties, he cannot follow the Way unless he be at peace.

And even then his capacity is beneath that of men of ancient times. Entering into the woods, ascending the mountains, *he* must have wherewithal to satisfy his hunger and to ward off the tempest. And so, by force of circumstance, he cannot escape what appear to be worldly desires. There is no help for this. It must be accepted. But it is nevertheless an unfair thing to say 'If such is the case, why retire from the world at all?' For a man who has entered on the Way, and is weary of the world, though it is true he is not free from desire, must not resemble those who retain their worldly power in the number of things he covets. What is the cost of a paper quilt, a hempen robe, a dish of food, a pottage made from herbs? His needs are simple, his desires readily appeased.

True, there are some who are ashamed of their garb, but however that may be, there is in most cases a withdrawal from evil and an approach to good.

Born as men, by that same token should we wish by all means

to escape from the world, for otherwise in what do we differ from the beasts, if we labour only to satisfy our appetites, and do not progress towards salvation?

59. He who proposes to devote himself to the great matters, however hard the wrench, must throw up, his purpose unachieved, those undertakings on which his heart is set.

If you start to think 'First I must finish off this, then I must get rid of that . . . people will laugh at me about so and so. I must assure my future, make proper provision – there is plenty of time before me. I have gone all these years, I can wait a little longer. There is no need for haste', and so on, then you will find that you are involved in a growing number of tasks you cannot quit, that there is no end to your affairs, and the day for making the change will never come.

Looking round, one sees that nearly all such as have a little feeling go through life more or less in this way.

Do men that are fleeing from a fire near at hand cry, 'Wait a while'? Wishful to save their lives, they are careless of shame, they cast away their treasure and escape.

Does existence wait on man? Nay! When the change comes, its onslaught is swifter even than that of fire or flood. It cannot be averted. At its approach, regret it though they may, the aged parent and the tender child alike must leave behind the grace of sovereigns and the love of fellow men.

60. In the monastery called Shinjōin there was a priest – an abbot – named Jōshin, who was a man of great wisdom. He was very fond of potatoes, of which he was wont to eat a great quantity. Even at his sermons he would keep at his knees a large bowl piled high with them, which he would eat as he expounded the scriptures. Whenever he suffered in body his treatment was to retire to his cell, taking of the finest potatoes what quantity he chose, and to eat of them more than ever. In this way he cured every sickness.

He never gave his potatoes to others to eat, but always ate them alone. Though he was very poor, when his superior died and left him 200 kan in money and his hermitage, he sold the hermitage for 100 kan, and the total sum of 300 kan he put aside for the purchase of potatoes. He entrusted the amount to a friend in the capital, and, drawing from it 10 kan at a time, bought for himself no stint of potatoes. When the money was exhausted it had been spent on potatoes and nothing else.

People said what a splendid example it was of true religion that such a poor man, on obtaining a sum of 300 kan, should dispose of it in this manner.

It was this abbot who, on seeing a certain priest, gave him the name *Shirōruri*, and when people asked what that might be, said, 'I do not know what it is myself. But if there is such a thing, then it must be like this priest's face.'

He was a man of handsome appearance and great strength; of enormous appetite; excelling in calligraphy and scholarship; and of eloquent speech. A leading light of his sect, he was much thought of in the temple, but, being an eccentric, who despised the world, he did always as he pleased and rarely as others wished. When attending to his offices at the temple, he would never at meals wait until others were served, but, as soon as his portion was placed before him, would finish it alone and leave the room.

He ate neither at the ordinary mealtimes nor at other fixed times, but when he was hungry, be it at midnight or daybreak. When drowsy he would retire even at noon, and would brook no disturbance, however important business might be afoot. Once awake, he would not sleep for several nights, but cheerfully walk round humming to himself.

Though of such an unusual nature he was disliked by no one, and everything was forgiven to him, doubtless by reason of his great virtue.

61. The dropping of *koshiki** when one of the Imperial ladies is delivered of a child is not a fixed custom, but a charm used when the afterbirth is stubborn. It is not done if the birth is easy. The custom came from the common people, and there is no authority for it.

The *koshiki* used are brought from the village of Ōhara. In pictures that have been preserved since ancient times one sees

* *Koshiki*: a basket for steaming rice. Read as *ko shiki* it signifies 'child cover', i.e. the placenta or afterbirth.

drawings of the dropping of these boxes when a child has been born in the house of a common person.

62. When Princess Ensei was a child she sent these lines as a message to the emperor.

> The letter for two
> The letter like a bull's horns
> A straight letter
> A bent letter
> And that's how I think of you!

meaning that she thought of him lovingly [i.e. 'koishiku' written こいしく].

63. The assembly of men at arms by the Shingon high priest during the palace rituals for the second week of the year is a precaution taken because once upon a time robbers broke in, and that is why all this business of palace-watchmen came about. As all appearances during the time of these observances are omens of events throughout the year, the employment of soldiers is inauspicious.

64. To ride in a carriage with five straps is not at all a personal privilege. Anybody can use them on obtaining high rank or office in his particular estate.

65. The head-dress of today has grown far higher than it used to be. I have heard it said that people who own old hatboxes use them nowadays with a new rim added.

66. The prince regent Okamoto once ordering the keeper of the hawks, Shimotsuke no Takekatsu, to take, as a gift to a distinguished person, a brace of birds which he had attached to a branch of full-blown red plum blossom, the latter said, 'I know no way of fixing birds to blossoms, nor have I ever heard of fixing two birds to one branch.' The prince made enquiries in his kitchen, and asked a number of people, and finally said to Takekatsu, 'Very well, go and present them attached as you think

proper', whereupon he attached a single bird to a plum branch bearing no blossom, and so presented it.

Takekatsu said, 'A branch of brushwood or plum tree should be used, either in bud or from which the blossom has fallen. The Goyō pine may also be used. The branches should be seven (or six will do) feet long, and cut to a point with two equal cuts, and the bird tied in the middle. There are two branches, one for the feet to rest on, and the other to attach the bird. This should be done in two places, with unsplit tendrils of the creeper *tsuzura*, the end being cut short, so as to reach as far as the long tail feathers, and bent into the shape of a bull's horns. Then, on the first morning of snow [in the year], the branch borne on the shoulder, the bird should be ceremoniously taken in at the middle gate. Following the stone pavement under the eaves, so as to leave no track in the snow, the bearer should pluck and twist into disorder the feathers just above the tail, and then lean the branch up against the balustrade of the mansion. If a gift [of clothes] is bestowed upon him, he should throw them over his shoulder, make a deep obeisance and withdraw. The bird must not be taken thus if the first snow is deep enough to hide the toe of the boot.

The reason for plucking the feathers is – since the hawk always attacks at this spot, above where the tail joins the body – probably to make it appear as if it has been caught by a hawk.

What can be the reason for not attaching birds to flowers? In the *Ise Monogatari* we find it said, where in the long [i.e. ninth] month a pheasant was attached to an artificial plum branch,

> It matters not what season of the year.
> For these are flowers plucked for thee, my lord.

From this it appears there is no objection to artificial flowers.

67. The two shrines at Kamo of Iwamoto and Hashimoto are those of the poets Ariwara no Narihira and Fujiwara no Sanekata. People as a rule confuse them, so one year when on a pilgrimage there, I stopped an old priest who was passing, and enquired. He said, 'They say that Sanekata's is the one which is reflected in the water flowing before the shrines, and as Hashimoto is nearer to the river that must be the one. There is a poem by the priest Yoshimizu,

Here lies the gentle Ariwara, who of old
Did love the moon and gaze upon the flowers,

which I have heard refers to the Iwamoto shrine. But you, Sir, I am sure, know far more about these things than I do.' I was much impressed by his courteous reply.

The lady-in-waiting to the cloistered empress Imadegawa, Lady Konoe, herself a poetess, used in her youth to compose a hundred stanzas, write them out in ink mixed from the water from before these two shrines, and then make offering thereof. She had a truly high reputation, many of her poems being often on people's lips, and she was a skilful writer of Chinese verses and introductions.

68. There was a certain man, a sort of local sheriff, in Tsukushi, who held that the radish was a cure for all evils, and every morning for years he ate two of them cooked.

One day, taking advantage of the absence of people from his residence, the enemy fell upon him, attacking from all sides, when suddenly two warriors appeared in the house, and fighting without any regard for their lives, drove them all back. Greatly mystified, he asked who they were that had been so good as to fight on his behalf, seeing that they did not belong to his household. Whereupon they said, 'We are the radishes which you have trusted and eaten every morning for so many years', and vanished.

Such virtue was there in his great faith.

69. The sage of Shosha was a man who by dint of continued reading of the *Lotus Sutra* had arrived at purity of the six senses.

Once, taking lodging while on a journey, he heard the bubbling noise of beans being cooked over a fire of their own husks, and the bubble-bubble said 'How can you who are related to us treat us so cruelly?' And the husks which were being burnt said crackle-crackle and replied, 'Are we doing this of our own accord? It is hard enough for us to be burned, but how can we help it? You must not be angry with us.'

70. At the Seishodō festival in the Gen'ō period, about the time that the lute Genshō was lost, the minister Kikutei played on [another famous lute, named] Bokuba. Having taken his place he felt for the bridges, but one of them fell off, so he fixed it on with some rice glue which he carried in the bosom of his robe. This dried up well while the offerings were being made, and thus an untoward incident was avoided. It was said that certain palace women, having some grudge or other against him, had got together and loosened the bridge, and then replaced it as before.

71. As soon as we hear a person's name we form in our minds a picture of his appearance; but when we come to see him, he is never the man whose face we had imagined.

I suppose we all feel, when we hear stories of ancient times, that the houses were more or less the same as people's houses nowadays, and think of the people as like people we see about us. And am I alone in having sometimes within me a feeling that words I have just heard, or things I have just seen, have happened once before – when, I cannot recollect, but none the less certainly have happened?

72. Disagreeable things are:
>Too much furniture in a living room.
>Too many pens on an inkstand.
>Too many images in a private shrine.
>Too many rocks, herbs, and trees in a garden
>Too many children in a house.
>Too many words when men meet.
>Too many vows in a prayer.

Things of which it is good to see plenty:
>Books in a book-case.
>Dust in a dust heap.

73. As a rule the tales which get abroad in the world are false – perhaps because the truth is not interesting enough?

People always exaggerate things. More so, when months and years have passed and the place is distant do they relate any story they please, or even it put down in writing, so that at last it becomes established fact.

Stupid people, who are ignorant of a particular subject, talk wildly of a person's skill in some accomplishment, and of his achievements therein, as if he were a god; but those who are acquainted with the subject do not put the least faith in them. Always what one sees turns out to be different from what one has heard.

When people speak at random, letting their tongues run on heedless of exposure, what they say is soon felt to be mere empty talk; and when a man, though he feels a story is untrue, repeats it as it was told to him, with a twitching about the nose, he does not actually tell a lie. The lie to be feared is one that a man tells with an air of truth, hesitating here and there as if not quite sure, and yet making all his details agree.

When flattering falsehoods are told about people, they do not take great pains to contradict them.

When a man listens to a falsehood which the whole company is enjoying, because he thinks it is no use for him alone to contradict, he is even made witness to its truth, and so at last the tale becomes quite established.

Anyhow, it is a world that is full of lies, and we shall make no mistake if we make up our minds that what we hear is really not at all strange and unusual but merely exaggerated in the telling.

The tales that people of the lower orders tell are all of the sort that astound the hearer. Well-bred people do not talk of marvellous matters.

Nevertheless, it does not follow that one should entirely disbelieve the miracles of gods and buddhas and the lives of the incarnations.

The fact is, to believe seriously in popular tales would be silly, to contradict them would be idle; and one had better on the whole appear to think them true, while entirely disbelieving and yet not casting doubt or ridicule upon them.

74. Gathered together like ants, hastening east and west, hurrying north and south; some lofty, some base; some young, some old; some going abroad, some returning home; lying down to sleep at night, rising in the morning – what is the business they are about? They never cease in their greed for life, in their pursuit of gain. What do they expect from this nourishment of the body? Only old age and death are certain. They come apace and are on us quicker than thought. What pleasure can there be while awaiting them? Those who have wandered from the Way do not fear them, because, sunk in greed for name and profit, they reck not of the journey they so soon must make. Fools think of them with sorrow, because they reflect on their own impermanence, and do not know the reason of change.

75. What do people mean when they complain of solitude? It is a good thing to be alone and undisturbed.

If you follow the world, then your heart is captured by defilements from without, and you are easily led astray. If you mix with men, your speech is agreeable to the ears of others, but it comes not from your own heart. You jest with them, you quarrel with them, now hating, now rejoicing, and there is no end thereto. A thousand decisions must be made, and loss and gain are ever present. Upon delusion follows drunkenness, and in drunkenness you dream. Such is the way of all men – hurrying, hastening, infatuate and blind.

Though not yet knowing the true Way, we may be said to find joy for a time in breaking loose from our ties, taking no part in affairs and giving the heart repose; and it is written in the *Moho Shih Kuan*, 'Put an end to all ties of livelihood, of society, of arts and of learning.'

76. When, at times of grief and rejoicing in the houses of the great and flourishing, folk go in numbers to pay their respects, one does not like to see priests and hermits mingling with them and asking for admission. Even though they have good reason for so doing, priests ought to keep aloof from the world.

77. I cannot tolerate one who has no concern therewith discussing familiarly matters which are the common talk of the day, or telling others, or enquiring in a familiar way, about things which do not concern him. Country hermits and priests in particular gossip and ask about people in the world, as if of their private affairs, until one wonders how they come to know so much.

Nor can I tolerate his spreading abroad the latest strange and fashionable sayings. The man is enviable who does not learn these until they have become commonplace.

78. When in the presence of a new acquaintance, to carry on a conversation in fragments, laughing and exchanging meaning looks with a companion who knows the phrases and names of things you commonly use, makes the stranger feel as if he understood nothing – this is ignorant behaviour, and a sure sign of ill-breeding.

79. One should never make a show of having a deep knowledge of any subject. Well-bred people do not talk in a superior way even about things that they have a good knowledge of. It is people who come from the country who offer opinions unasked, as though versed in all manner of accomplishments. Of course there are some among them who have a really enviable knowledge, but it is their air of self-conceit which is so stupid.

It is a fine thing when a man who thoroughly understands a subject is unwilling to open his mouth, and only speaks when he is questioned.

80. Every man likes doing those things which are foreign to his calling. A priest learns the art of war, while soldiers on our frontiers do not know the way to draw a bow. They pretend to know the Buddhist law, they indulge in linking verses and playing music, although they are more despised for these accomplishments than for stupidity in their own profession.

And it is not only priests. Generally, among nobles and courtiers up to the very highest, there are numbers who are fond of arms. 'You may fight a hundred battles, and win a hundred battles, but it is still hard to establish warlike fame.' For this reason: any man is soldier enough to crush the foe when fortune favours him, but war is a profession where he cannot make his name until, his forces exhausted, his weapons at an end, he seeks death at the hands of the foe rather than surrender. So long as he is living, he cannot boast of warlike fame.

What then does it profit, unless one is of a military family, to devote oneself to conduct removed from human principles and approaching that of the beasts?

81. Paintings and inscriptions on doors and screens drawn with a clumsy brush impress one rather with the poor taste of the master of the house than with their own ugliness; and generally, a man's belongings will betray the inferiority of their owner's character.

Not, indeed, that one need have such very good things. What I refer to is the fondness for making things ugly and vulgar so that they shall be durable, or the addition of useless ornament so that they shall be curious.

What one wants are things with an air of age, not showy and expensive, but of good quality.

82. 'It is a pity that thin cloth covers of scrolls soon wear out,' said someone to Ton'a, who replied, 'It is only when the covers are torn top and bottom and the mother-of-pearl has fallen out of the ends of the roller that a volume looks well.' Whereby one perceives him to be a man of excellent taste.

Some people dislike to see a complete set of writings – sketches and so on – of which all the volumes are not alike. But Bishop Kōyu said (it seems to me very admirably), 'It is only a person of poor understanding who wishes to arrange things in complete sets. It is incompleteness that is desirable.' In everything regularity is bad. To leave a thing unfinished gives interest, and makes for lengthened life. They say that even in building the palace an unfinished place is always left. In the writings of the ancients, inner and outer [i.e. Buddhist and non-Buddhist], there are many missing chapters and parts.

83. The minister of the left, the lay-priest of Chikurin'in, might without any difficulty have become prime minister, but he saw nothing extraordinary in that, and therefore, stopping at the post of minister of the left, he entered the priesthood.

The minister of the left Tōin much admired this, and himself was without desire to become premier.

There is a phrase, 'the regret of the mounting dragon'. The moon waxes and then wanes. When the prime is reached then comes decline. In all things, where there is no room for advance decay is at hand.

84. When Fa-hsien went over to India he is said to have wept at the sight of a fan from his native land, and to have desired Chinese food when he lay sick; and someone hearing this said, 'How could such a man disgrace himself by displaying such weakness in a foreign country!' Whereupon Kōyu cried 'Nay! An excellent, feeling man!' Which seems to me an admirable remark, and unlike a priest.

85. The hearts of men not being pure, they are not without falsehood, but there is no reason why there should not be some who are by nature honest. It is the way of the world that those who are not themselves upright look with envy on the wisdom of others. At times, some of the very ignorant will look on a wise man with hatred, and revile him, saying, 'Aiming at great profit he refuses small profit, because he hopes to make a name by dressing in false colours.' But this very abuse shows that their heart is different from his. Theirs is the nature of the lowest ignorance, which is unchangeable, and they would not refuse to lie, even for small profit.

Even for a short space you should not imitate folly. If you run down the road in imitation of a madman, you are a madman. If you kill a man in imitation of an evildoer, you are an evildoer. To follow the example of the thousand league steed is to be of its kind. To copy the sage Shun is to be of his company. Even a false imitation of wisdom must be reckoned as wisdom.

86. Koretsugu no Chūnagon was a man richly endowed with poetical talent. He was a life-long devotee, and lodged with a temple priest, Bishop En'i, constantly reading the scriptures. In the Bumpō period [1317-19], when En'i's temple Miidera was burnt, he came upon him and said 'Your Reverence was a *tera-hōshi* [a priest of Miidera], but now there is no *tera* [temple] we must call you *hōshi* [priest; but also, one who regrets fire]. A very witty remark.

87. One should be careful how one gives drink to one's inferiors.

A man who lived in Uji was on intimate terms with a very accomplished priest, a hermit called Gugakubō, whose brother-in-law he was. One day he sent his horse to fetch him, and the priest set wine before the groom, saying 'We have a long way to go, take a drink.' He gulped down cup after cup, and then, girding on his sword, set out escorting the priest in high feather.

As they went along, they encountered near Kobata some Nara priests with a large train of soldiers. The groom confronted them, saying, 'This looks suspicious – here at nightfall among the hills. Stop!' He drew his sword, whereupon the others all drew theirs or fixed arrows to their bows. Gugakubō, rubbing his palms together, cried, 'Sirs, he is drunk, and out of his real mind. Pray forgive him, though he does not deserve it.' So they all derided him and passed on.

Then the man, turning to Gugakubō, said, 'Now, Sir, see what you have done. I wished to perform a feat of valour, and you have made me draw my sword in vain', and in a passion, he cruelly slashed and cut him down. Then as he cried 'Robbers, robbers', a crowd of villagers turned out and came towards him, and he, saying '*I* am the Robber', rushed at them, cutting all around him till a number of them together wounded him and bound him as he lay prostrate.

The horse, splashed with blood, ran to its home on the Uji highroad. Its master, dismayed at the sight, sent men running out, who found Gugakubō insensible on Kuchinashihara and carried him back. He just escaped with his life, but was so hurt by cuts about the loins that he became a cripple.

88. A certain person had a copy of the *Wakan Rōei Shū* said to be in the handwriting of Ono no Tōfu [896-966], of which someone said, 'As it is a family heirloom of yours, there can hardly be any mistake; but it is very curious that Tōfu should have written out what Fujiwara no Kintō selected. Surely the periods are different.'* The owner, hearing this, said, 'In that case it must be very rare indeed,' and treasured it more than ever.

89. They say that in the heart of the mountains there lives a beast which eats men, known as the *nekomata*. A priest named Something-amidabutsu, a maker of linked verses, who lived near the Gyōgan temple, hearing someone remark, 'Though this is not a mountain district, even hereabouts cats have been known to grow after a time into *nekomata* and carry people away,' thought to himself, 'A man who walks about alone ought to take care.' Just at this time, returning home alone after having been at verse-making until late at night, what should suddenly approach his feet near the edge of a small stream, but one of these same *nekomata* of which he had heard. It leapt on to him, and made to bite him about the throat. Frightened out of his wits, he had no strength to resist, his legs gave way, and he tumbled into the stream, shrieking 'Help! Help! A *nekomata*, a *nekomata*!' People ran out from their houses with torches to see what had happened, and there found the priest, who was well known by sight in those parts. Wondering what had happened, they picked him up out of the stream. He had won a prize at the verse-making, and his fan, his box, and other things, which he carried in his bosom, had fallen into the water. He crept into his house as if he had had a wonderful escape. It was his own dog, which had recognized its master in the dark, and jumped up at him!

90. There was in the service of a priest who was a counsellor a boy named Otozurumaru who knew, and frequently visited, one Lord Yasura. One day, on his return, his master said, 'Where have you been?' And he replied, 'I have been to Lord Yasura's.' On being asked, 'Is this Lord Yasura a [lay] man or a priest?' he

* Kintō, the work's compiler, was born in 966.

replied, hiding his face with his sleeves, 'I do not know. I did not see his head.'*

How could he have not seen his head?

92. A person learning archery takes in his hand both arrows. The teacher says: 'Beginners ought not to hold two arrows. They rely on their second arrow and are careless about the first. You ought each time to think, without any idea of missing and hitting, "*This* is the shot which counts." '

One may think, 'Surely, with two arrows only, a man will not be careless in the teacher's presence.' But, though a man does not know when his own care relaxes, the teacher does know, and this counsel extends to all things.

People who are studying think at night, 'There is tomorrow.' Tomorrow they think, 'There is tonight', and so they go on, always meaning to work diligently. Nay, more – does not the attention relax even in moment of time? Why is it so hard to do a thing *Now*, at the moment when one thinks of it.

93. Someone said, 'A man has an ox to sell. A buyer comes and says, "Tomorrow I will give you the money and take the ox." In the night the ox dies. He who was to buy has gained; he who was to sell has lost.'

A bystander, hearing this, remarked, 'It is true that the owner of the ox suffered loss. But again he gained a great deal. For this reason, that all living things are ignorant of the nearness of death. It was so with this ox, and men are the same. It happened that the ox died. It happened that its owner lived. One day of life is weightier than ten thousand pieces of gold. The price of an ox is lighter than a feather. A man who gains ten thousand pieces of gold and loses a farthing cannot be said to have suffered loss.'

Whereupon everyone scoffed at him, saying, 'That argument cannot be confined to the owner of the ox.'

Further he said that since men hate death they ought to love life. Why then do they not daily take pleasure in the joy of existence? The foolish, forgetting this pleasure, laboriously seek

---

* If his head was shaven, he would have been a priest.

other pleasures. They forget this treasure, and rashly covet other treasures. But their desires are never fulfilled. While they live, they take no pleasure in life; when they come near dying, they fear death – which is contrary to this reasoning. It is not because they do not fear death, but because they forget the nearness of death that men do not rejoice in life. One might say that he has grasped the true principle who is unconcerned with the manifestations of life and death.

When he said this people scoffed at him more than ever.

94. A court official bearing an imperial letter once dismounted on meeting the prime minister Tokiwai, who was on his way to attend at the palace. The prime minister afterwards said, 'Such-and-such an officer dismounted from his horse while bearing an imperial letter. How can such a man serve his Majesty!' and dismissed him.

An imperial letter should be presented [even] to a superior while on horseback. The bearer should not dismount.

95. I once asked a learned man where, in turning [the lid of] a box, the attachment of the cords should be, and he replied, 'There are two opinions. One is to attach them to the mount, one to the roller. There is no objection to either. In book-boxes it is, as a rule, on the right; in hand-boxes it is usual to attach to the roller.'

96. There is a plant called *menamomi*. If a man who has been bitten by a viper rubs this plant in his hands and applies it, he will be cured forthwith. One should learn to recognize it.

97. There is no end to the number of cases where a thing wastes and damages the thing to which it belongs. The body has lice, the house has rats, the nation has robbers. The common man has goods, the sage has righteousness, the priest has the [Buddhist] law.

98. The following are things which I remember as having pleased me when I read a book in which were written down the sayings of venerable sages, called *Ichigon Hōdan*.

i   Things of which you think 'Shall I do it, or shall I not?' are for the most part better left undone.

ii   A man who thinks of the life to come should not possess one *miso* tub, and it is wrong for him to have even a good prayer-book and image for his own use.

iii   The hermit lives so that he wants for nothing by having nothing. Of such is the very highest excellence.

iv   The man of high rank should become as one of low degree, the wise man ignorant, the rich poor, the capable incapable.

v   This and none other is to desire to enter in the way of Buddha – to give over one's business, to take no thought of the things of this world. Such is the foremost way.

There were other things, but I do not remember them.

99. The prime minister Horikawa was a handsome man, in very enviable circumstances, and much given to extravagance in all things. His son, Lord Mototoshi, he made chief of the court police, and in the course of his duties, he noticed archive chests in his office which he said were unsightly, and ordered them to be remade in a more elegant way.

The officers who understood ancient matters pointed out, 'These chests date from the earliest ages, and nobody knows their beginnings. Such government property, after successive generations, being old and dilapidated, becomes a pattern for us and can hardly be renewed.' And so he gave up his intention.

100. The prime minister Koga, when on duty in the palace, wished to drink some water, and the palace-servants offered him an earthenware vessel. But he said, 'Bring me a wooden ladle', and drank from the ladle.

101. A certain man, who was performing the functions of master of the ceremonies at the Investiture of Ministers, attended at court without taking the imperial edicts from the palace writers. It was beyond measure a breach of etiquette, but he could not go back and fetch them, and he was much concerned what to do, when Yasutsuna, palace writer of the sixth grade, spoke to one of the court-ladies, and got her to pass them to him unobserved. This was very admirable.

102. When the lay priest Koga Mitsutada was master of the ceremonies at the Expulsion of Evil, and was being told by the minister of the left, Dōin, what the procedure would be, he said, 'The wisest way is to get instruction from Matagorō.' This Matagorō was an old soldier of the palace guard, well versed in public ceremonies. Once when Lord Konoe, taking his place at audience, had forgotten his kneeling-mat and summoned a secretary to his side, Matagorō, who was lighting fires at the time, whispered unobserved [to the secretary], 'I suspect his lordship wants a kneeling-mat' – which was very well done.

103. Once when the retired emperor Go-Uda and his courtiers were playing at riddles, there came to them the physician Tadamori; whereon the chamberlain, Kin'akira, made this riddle: 'Why is Tadamori not a native of this country?' The answer was, 'Because he is a *karaheishi*.'* At this they all joined in laughter, and he withdrew in anger.

104. A certain person, going to visit a woman at a time when she had to sequester herself and was living in solitude shut up in a house away from the sight of men, went secretly thither by the dim light of an early moon. A dog challenged him noisily, and there came out a serving woman who said, 'Whence comest thou?' And he was soon asked within and entered. There was something gloomy about the place which made him anxious,

* Tadamori was also the name of a famous leader of the Taira warrior clan. 'Karaheishi' can be understood as both 'unreal Taira warrior' and 'Chinese medicine bottle'.

wondering how she passed her time. He stood for a time on the crazy planked floor [outside the room], until someone with a youthful voice said in a quiet tone, 'Come this way', and he entered through a narrow sliding doorway that stood open.

Within, it had a far from cheerless air. There was a pleasantly dim light in the distance, enough to show the ornaments in the room, and a perfume which somehow seemed to belong to the place. She lived then in very enviable wise.

'Make the gate fast' – 'It's going to rain' – 'The gentleman's carriage in the gateway, and his people in such and such a place' – she says to the servants, and they whisper, 'Tonight, forsooth, we shall sleep peacefully.' And though 'tis said in secret, they, being not far off, are just overheard.

Now he asks her in detail all that has happened of late, and behold, the cock crows deep in the night! So they pass on to earnest discourse, ranging from the past into the future, until now the cock crows long and loud with a brave note, that sounds as if the day were breaking; but as it is not the sort of place where there is need for haste here late in the night, he delays awhile. At length the chinks in the shutters lighten, and then, saying not-to-be-forgotten things, he rises and departs.

Even now, when passing that way, he recalls that bright and lovely dawn in May, the tree tops and the gardens everywhere all wonderful and green, and looks back until the great oak is out of sight.

105. Against the north side of the house, where the still unmelted snow had frozen hard, a carriage was drawn up, and the hoar frost glistened on its shafts. The daybreak moon shone clear, though there were dark corners; and yonder on the gallery of the unfrequented Great Hall one who did not look a common man was seated with a woman on the rail. They were engaged in talk which, whatever it may have been about, seemed as if it would never end. She appeared to be of excellent carriage and figure, and the way in which there came a sudden waft of vague perfume was very pleasing. Delightful, too, to watch their gestures and to catch now and again fragments of their talk.

106. The priest Shōkū of Mount Kōya once, when on his way up to Kyōto, was met on a narrow path by a woman riding on a horse, whose groom, through clumsy leading, caused the sage's horse to fall into the ditch. The sage scolded him most angrily, saying 'What extraordinary rudeness is this? See here! There are four grades of disciples – a *bikuni* [nun] is lower than a *biku* [monk], an *ubasoku* [male lay believer] is lower than a *bikuni* [nun], an *ubai* [female lay believer] is lower than an *ubasoku* [male lay believer]. This is monstrous conduct, for a mere *ubai* [female lay believer] to drive a *biku* [monk] into the ditch!' The groom said 'I cannot make out what you are saying, Sir', and at this his Reverence, fuming still more, shouted: 'What sayest thou, fellow without doctrine or practice?' And then, looking as if he felt he had used words beyond measure insulting, turned his horse round and fled!

Surely a very noble dispute!

107. In the time of the cloistered emperor Kameyama, some frolicsome court ladies, holding that there are very few men who can at once give a fair answer to a question put by a woman, used, whenever young men came to see them, to ask as a test, 'Have you heard the nightingale?'

A certain counsellor replied, 'Such an insignificant person as myself cannot hear it!' The home minister Horikawa said, 'I believe I heard it at Iwakura.' 'There is nothing wrong with that,' they criticised, 'but "insignificant person" and so on will never do.'

It was said of the former regent Jōdoji that it was because he had been well instructed in his youth by Princess Anki, on the principle that a man should always be brought up so as not to be laughed at by women, that his manner of speech was so good.

Yamashina, minister of the left, used to say he felt most bashful and ill at ease when even a common serving woman looked at him.

If there were no women in the world, no one would ever be careful of his dress or his headgear.

One would think that the character of these women, before whom people are so ashamed, was a very fine thing indeed, yet a woman's disposition is always crooked.

The trait of selfishness is strong. Greed is powerful. They do not know the reason of things, and their hearts are quickly inclined to error. Their speech is clever. They will not reply even to a harmless question. Out of discretion, one might think, but no! For, on the other hand, they will unasked utter the most silly things in their talk.

Deep in deceit and lies, one would think them superior to men in cunning. Yet they do not see that they are found out in the end.

Dishonest and yet unskilful – this is woman. One must be infatuated indeed to wish to please her, and to gain her approval. Why therefore be ashamed before women? If there were a wise woman she would be cold and forbidding. It is only when, mastered by infatuation, men are attached to women that they find them tender and pleasing.

108. No man is careful of small moments of time. Is this through fullness of knowledge or through foolishness? Speaking for those whose neglect is due to foolishness, one may say that a tenth of a penny is but a trifling sum; and nevertheless, it is by the accumulation of these that a poor man will become a rich man. A merchant's care for his pennies is keen. So, though we may not perceive the passing of the moments, yet as they progress unceasingly, of a sudden we reach the term of life.

Therefore the wise man will not be careful of far-off days and months, but rather careful lest the present moment pass unprofitably.

Should there come one to you and announce that tomorrow you would without fail lose your life, until the close of today on what would you set your hope, what task would you undertake?

What is the difference between this today that we are living and such a season?

Out of a single day much time is lost in eating, drinking, sleeping, talking and walking, that cannot be done without. Foolish indeed it is, in the little space there is to spare from these – in doing unprofitable things, saying unprofitable things and thinking unprofitable things – not only to pass the hours, but to spend the days, to consume the months, and so to live a whole life.

Though Hsieh Ling-yün was a transcriber of the sutras, his mind was always fixed on thoughts of clouds and wind [i.e. poetry], and therefore Hui-yüan would not admit him to the Society of the White Lotus.

Even for a time to be without this [conviction] is to be as a dead man. And if one enquires why one should be so grudging of time, the answer is: let him who will withdraw, withdraw; let him who will practise, practise; having no care within, no business without.

109. A man who was famous as a tree climber would make a person he was teaching climb a tall tree to cut the topmost branches, but never said a word when he appeared to be in great danger. When he was getting down, and had reached the height of the eaves above the ground, he would call out, 'Don't make a false step. Come down carefully.'

Someone said, 'Why do you say that now he has got so far? He might even jump down now.' To this he replied, 'That is so. When a man feels dizzy, on a perilous branch, he is in fear himself, and I say nothing. Mistakes always happen when an easy place is reached.'

Though he was but a man of humble station, what he said was in accordance with the teaching of the sages.

It is the same with a football. It is when a difficult kick has been made, and the next appears easy, that one is sure to miss, they say.

110. A man who was known for his skill at backgammon, on being asked what his method of play was, replied, 'You should never play to win, but so as not to lose. Think what moves will be quickest beaten, avoid making them, and make whatever move will take most time to beat, even by a square.'

In learning any accomplishment, in controlling one's own conduct, and in governing a nation, the same rule applies.

111. This saying of a certain sage struck me as very fine, and remained in my ears: 'I think it is a greater wickedness than even the four crimes [murder, theft, adultery, lying] and the five offences [patricide, matricide, murder of an arhat, brewing mischief between priests, letting the blood of a buddha] for a man to delight in spending day and night at games of checkers and backgammon.'

112. What single worldly observance is there which cannot be avoided? If you comply with the demands of society and persist in regarding them as inevitable, then your desires increase, your person suffers, and your mind is never free from care. You spend your whole life hindered by a succession of trifling duties, and anon it comes to an unprofitable close.

The night falls, the way is long, and our life already tottering. It is time to cast loose all our ties. We must not keep faith. We must not consider ceremony. People who are not of this mind may call us mad, but there is no truth in them. They may think us heartless, but we are not troubled that they revile us, nor will we listen to their praise.

113. When a man over forty who has leanings to lewdness does his best to conceal them, there is nothing more to be said; but when it shows in his speech and he jests about men and women [in general] and the affairs of [particular] persons – it is indeed unpleasant and unseemly.

Things which are unpleasant to see and disagreeable to hear are: an old man mixing with young people and trying to be funny; a person of no importance talking as if he were very intimate with people of reputation; and a man of poor circumstances fond of feasting, making a great shine to entertain guests.

114. Once, when the minister of Imadegawa was proceeding to Saga, Saiōmaru whipped up the minister's bulls in a place where there was running water near Arisugawa, so that they splashed up a deal of water on to the front boards of the carriage. Tamenori who was in attendance at the rear of the carriage, said, 'You young rascal! What do you mean by whipping up his Lordship's bulls in such a

place? 'At this the minister himself grew angry, and exclaiming, 'Thou, canst thou drive a carriage better than Saiōmaru? Rascal thyself!' knocked Tamenori's head up against the carriage.

This well-known Saiōmaru was a servant of Uzumasa and keeper of the oxen in his household. Among the women employed by Lord Uzumasa was one called Hizasachi [strong-kneed], one called Kototsuchi [round-like-a-mallet], one Hōhara [big-bellied] and another Otoushi [last-born].*

115. At a place called Shukugahara a large number of *boroboro* [wandering priests] were assembled, reciting the prayer to Amida, when there entered from without another who said, 'Is there among you a priest named Irooshi, Sirs?' The reply came forth from their midst, 'Irooshi is here. Who is it that speaks?' 'I am called Shirabonji. My master so-and-so was, I have heard, killed in the eastern provinces by a wandering priest named Irooshi. I wish to have the honour of meeting that gentleman, and, avenging my master's death. That is why I ask.' Irooshi replied, 'Nobly asked, sir! I did do such a thing. But an encounter here would pollute this place of devotion. Let us meet in the river-bed in front, therefore.' 'I am humbly grateful.' 'Pray let not the company present assist either party. If too many should get into trouble, it would hinder the performance of the service of Buddha.'

Having thus arranged matters, the two went out to the river bed, where they pierced one another to their hearts' content, and died together.

They say that formerly there were no *boroboro*, but they began in recent times, with men who were named Boronji, Bonji, Kanji and so on.

Wilful and determined, they appear to be devoted to the way of Buddha, but they make strife and quarrel their business. Though dissolute and cruel in appearance they think lightly of death, and cling not at all to life. The bravery of such men having impressed me, I set this down as it was related to me.

* All names apropriate to oxen.

116. The people of ancient times never went out of their way to give names to shrines and temples – or to things in general, for that matter. They just simply named them according to the facts.

Nowadays names sound as if people had racked their brains to show their cleverness, which is altogether wrong. In personal names, too, it is a useless thing to use characters which one rarely sees. A desire for curious things, a fondness for uncommon opinions, is a sure characteristic of people of shallow understanding.

117. There are seven sorts of people whom it is bad to have as friends:

> First, men of high rank and power.
> Second, young people.
> Third, strong people who are never ill.
> Fourth, people fond of wine.
> Fifth, fierce and bold military men.
> Sixth, people whose speech is false.
> Seventh, greedy people.

Good friends are three.
> Friends who make gifts.
> Doctors.
> Friends who are wise.

119. A fish called *katsuo*, in the sea near Kamakura, is unequalled in that part of the country, and has been much prized of late. The old men of Kamakura say, 'Up till our young days, this fish was never set before people of standing. Even the servants did not eat the head, but cut it off and threw it away.'

In these latter times, even such things as these have penetrated as far as the very highest.

120. We could do without anything from China except drugs. As for books, they are spread all over this country, and we could copy them. It is a foolish thing for ships from China to make the perilous journey over here, crammed with cargoes of useless things.

Is it not written, moreover, 'Neither treasuring things from afar, nor prizing jewels that are rare'?

121. Of domestic animals, horses and oxen, though it is a pity to have to keep them in irksome bondage, cannot be done without, so there is no help for it; dogs, too, are superior to men in the task of watching and defending, and are therefore necessary; though, as every house has one, it is as well not to purchase one specially.

All other birds and beasts are useless. When beasts that run are shut in houses and tied with chains, or birds that fly are thrust in cages and their wings clipped, then they long for the clouds and think of the hills and fields. They never cease from grief; and who that has a heart can take pleasure in feelings which, if he himself were to suffer them, would be unbearable? He whose eyes are delighted by torture of living things has a heart like [the cruel emperors] Chieh and Chou.

Wang Tzu-yu was a lover of birds. He watched them sporting among the trees, and made them the companions of his walks abroad. He did not capture and torture them. It is written that 'in a state neither should strange birds nor curious beasts be kept.'

122. Of a man's abilities first comes knowledge of the teachings of the sages, by a clear understanding of literature. Next is handwriting, which should be studied, even though not as an object in itself, as an aid to learning.

Next should be learned the art of medicine. Without medicine, a man cannot care for his own body, nor help others, nor perform his duties to parents and his lord.

Next come archery and the riding of a horse, from among the six accomplishments, and they certainly must be given attention.

A knowledge of letters, arms and medicine cannot in truth be done without; and a man who will learn these cannot be said to be an idle person.

'Food is man's heaven', and it must be accounted a great virtue in a man to know how to prepare well-tasting food.

Next is handicraft, which has a thousand uses.

Beyond these, too many accomplishments are a source of shame to high and low. Skill in poetry, talent for music are fine and admirable qualities; but though sovereign and subject may prize them, nowadays a condition of things has been reached where it would seem foolish to [expect to] govern a state by their means. Though gold is superior, it cannot equal iron in the multitude of its uses.

123. A man who spends his time doing unprofitable things must be called both foolish and wicked. There are many things to be done which may not be neglected, for country and for king. The leisure that is left from these is little enough. It must be cherished.

Of these things which a man must perforce attend to for his own person, first comes his food, second his clothing, and third his dwelling.

The chief business of man is none other than these three. To live peacefully, without being hungry, without being cold, without being harmed by wind and rain – this is happiness.

Nevertheless, to all men there comes sickness, and the sorrow brought by the attacks of sickness is hard to bear. The art of healing should not be forgotten.

Not to have got these four things, together with music, is to be poor. Not to be lacking in them is to be rich. To seek to obtain more than these four is luxury. These four things, for one who is frugal, who can say that they do not suffice?

124. A fox will bite people. In the Horikawa mansion an attendant lying asleep had his leg bitten by a fox. Once at the Ninnaji temple three foxes flew at and bit a priest who was passing at night in front of the main temple. He drew his sword and in warding them off stabbed two of the foxes. One he stabbed to death, and two escaped. The priest was bitten in several places, but was not dangerously hurt.

125. Once, those left behind [by one who died] invited a certain holy man to perform the forty-ninth-day ceremonies. So beautiful was his exposition of the Buddhist law that everyone shed tears. After he had left, those who had heard him were talking together, remarking that today they had been more than usually impressed; whereupon someone replied, 'Why, of course – since he's so like a Chinese dog.' Meaning that the priest was so like a Chinese dog that he must have all the Chinese learning.

Whereupon their feeling of wonder vanished, and they were all amused.

What a way of praising a priest !

Again, so said someone, for one who wishes to persuade another to take wine, first to drink himself and then to offer it to the other is as if one were about to cut another with a sword. In each case we have an edged weapon. Taking it up, and first cutting our own head off, we cannot wound another. Getting drunk first oneself, and lying down, others will hardly take any.

This was very funny. Had he made a trial with a sword, I wonder.

126. Someone once said, 'When one party has lost heavily at gambling, and proposes to stake his all, the other party should not play. He should recognize that the moment has come when the luck will turn and his opponent win time after time. A good gambler is one who knows when this moment has come.'

127. If there is no advantage in changing a thing it is better not to change it.

128. The counsellor Masafusa was a good man, of fine understanding. His Majesty the retired emperor had the intention, indeed, of making him a general, but about this time, someone attached to his Majesty's person said, 'I saw a very evil thing just now.' 'What was that?' enquired his Majesty, and the reply was, 'I saw, through a hole in the fence, Masafusa cut off the legs of a live dog, in order to feed his hawks.' His Majesty was disgusted, and he did not promote Masafusa.

Though it was strange of such a personage to possess hawks, the story of the dog's legs was without foundation. The slander was a great pity, but his Majesty's displeasure on hearing of such a thing was noble.

Those who find it a pleasant sport to kill living things, or to hunt them or make them fight, are akin to beasts of prey.

If we carefully observe the condition of all beasts and birds, down even to the small insects, we see that they love their children and are fond of their parents; that male and female consort together; that they feel jealousy and anger; that their desires are manifold; that they cherish their bodies and grudge their lives – all much more so than men, and this entirely because they have no reason. Is it not pitiful indeed to give pain to such as these or to deprive them of their lives?

A man without the sentiment of mercy towards every single thing that has feeling acts contrary to the principal of humanity.

129. Though the joys, the angers, the griefs and the pleasures of older people are all empty and unreal, yet who is there that does not firmly believe them to be something real and actual?

More harm is done to a man by afflicting his mind than by hurting his body.

Sickness, too, is chiefly come by through the mind. Sickness from without is rare. Though there is often no effect when a man takes drugs to make him sweat, let him once have some cause for shame or fear, and he will most surely drip with sweat – and this, it must be marked, is the work of the mind. We are not without the example of him who inscribed the tablet at the top of a lofty tower and became a white-haired man!

130. There is nothing better than to refrain from contention; to yield oneself, and to follow others; to put oneself last and others first.

Those who like games where the players compete for victory do so because of the pleasure they get from winning. But if a man rejoices because his skill exceeds another's, it follows that he will find it unpleasant to lose. Still less will he take pleasure in playing a game to rejoice another by losing himself.

To get amusement oneself, making others feel dissatisfied, is contrary to morality.

Even when jesting among friends, one man will hoodwink and deceive another, taking pleasure in his superior knowledge. This again is against propriety. Many a long continued hatred, of every sort, is thus first formed, arising out of some convivial gathering. All these are the fault of a love of contention.

If you have a mind to excel others, then let your only desire be for learning, that you may excel them in wisdom. For if you study the Way, then you will learn not to be proud of your virtues, and not to contend with your fellows.

It is the power of learning alone that makes men give up high office and throw away great profit.

131. The poor think social virtue requires money, and the old think it requires strength.

To know your own condition, and to refrain immediately from what is beyond your reach, is wisdom. If you are not allowed to do so, that is the fault of others; but if you persistently strive, not knowing your condition, that is your own fault. If a poor man does not know his condition, he steals. If a man of impaired strength does not know his condition, he falls sick.

132. The name Toba New Road was not given after the Toba Pavilion was built, but is an old name. In the records of Prince Shigeaki, it is written that the voice of his Highness Motoyoshi was of such excellence, when he was making the address to the throne on the first day of the year, that he was heard from the Daikokuden to the Toba New Road.

133. In the imperial bedchamber the pillow is to the east. The pillow is placed to the east in order to receive the influence of light. Confucius too lay with his head to the east.

In the arrangement of bedchambers in some mansions, however, a southward pillow is common.

Emperor Shirakawa used to sleep towards the north. The north is inauspicious. Moreover Ise is to the south, and people asked how it was his Majesty put the direction of the great shrine behind him. But in worshipping the great shrine from afar the emperor faces to the south-east, not the south.

134. A certain *samādhi* priest of the Hokke temple of the cloistered emperor Takakura once took a mirror and looked carefully at his face. So grieved was he at the ugliness and meanness of his own appearance that even a mirror was hateful to him, and afterwards for a long time he was afraid of a mirror, and never took one in his hand. He did not mix at all with others, but

kept in seclusion, only performing his duties in the temple. Such is a tale I was told, and thought it a very rare story.

Even those who have an air of being wise judge of others only, and do not know themselves. It cannot be in reason to know others and not to know oneself. Therefore one who knows himself may be said to be a man who has knowledge.

Though our looks be unpleasing, we do not know it. We do not know that our hearts are foolish. We do not know that our skill is poor. We do not know that our station is lowly. We do not know that we grow old in years. We do not know that sickness attacks us. We do not know that death is near. We do not know that we have not attained the Way we follow. We do not know what evil is in our own persons, still less what calumny comes from without.

But, you may say, our looks can be seen in a mirror, years may be known by counting, and we are not unaware of our character – though because it cannot be helped, it appears as if we were unaware thereof. Nevertheless you are not told to change your looks, nor to make young your years. If you know your unskilfulness, why do you not withdraw? If you know you have grown old, why do you not live in tranquil ease? If you know your behaviour is foolish, why should your thought be not your deed?

It is ever a shame for a man to mix in company where he is not liked and welcomed. Ugly in looks and base in feeling, to take service; lacking knowledge, to mix with great minds; having meagre accomplishments, to sit beside men of parts; with snow-white head, to go among those in their prime. Nay, more! To desire what cannot be attained, to grieve at what cannot be compassed, to await what will not come, to be dreaded by others, to flatter others – this is not a shame put on a man by others, but it is he who shames himself, drawn on by his own greedy heart.

And why greed never ceases is because men never surely know that now and here has come the great occasion, the end of life.

135. One Sukesue, a lay-priest and counsellor, meeting the prime minister Tomouji Chūjō, said to him 'Whatever question you ask me I will answer. No matter what.'

'I wonder,' said Tomouji. 'Well,' was the reply, 'pray dispute with me!' 'Of serious matters I have not even a scrap of learning,

so it is useless to question you concerning such. I will do myself
the honour of asking about some trifle, some piece of nonsense,
which I do not understand.'

'The more so if it is some small matter of our own country.
Whatever it be I will make it clear to you.'

The retinue and the women in waiting thought this a diverting
dispute, the more so if the discussion should take place before
his Majesty. So they arranged that he who was defeated should
provide a feast, and they were summoned together to the
Presence. Then Tomouji said, 'There is something which I have
been used to hear from my youth up, but have never understood.
What is the meaning of the words "*Umanokitsuryōkitsuninowo-
kanakakuboreirikurendo*"? I pray you tell me.'

The counsellor was at a loss. 'This is nonsense,' he said, 'and
there is no need to answer.'

'Yes,' replied Tomouji, 'but did I not arrange with you that,
since of course I have no deep learning, I should ask you some
piece of nonsense?'

So the counsellor lost; and, they said, had to pay his forfeit most
handsomely.

136. The physician Atsushige, when in attendance on the late
emperor-in-retirement, was once asked by his Majesty, when his
meal was served, what was the efficacy, and how to write the
names, of the various dishes. He replied from memory, and said,
'I pray your Majesty will deign to compare this with the herbal
Honsō. I think there will not be a single mistake.' At that moment
the Rokujō home minister, Minamoto no Arifusa, entered. 'Here
is a chance to learn something,' said Arifusa. 'Now, what is the
radical in the character for *salt*?'

'It is the radical *earth*,' said Atsushige.

'Ah! Now the extent of your talent is already clear! That will
do. There is nothing to admire.' At which words there was a
burst of laughter, and Arifusa withdrew.*

---

* The radical earth is only used in the vulgarly abbreviated form of the
character.

137. Are we only to look at flowers in full bloom, at the moon when clear?

Nay, to look out on the rain and long for the moon, to draw the blinds and not to know the passing of the spring – these arouse even deeper feelings. There is much to be seen in young boughs about to flower, in gardens strewn with withered blossom. Where in the titles of verses it is written 'On going to see the blossoms, but they had too quickly fallen and passed away', or 'On being prevented from going to see the blossoms', are the verses inferior to those written 'On seeing the blossoms'?

Men are wont to regret that the moon has waned or that the blossoms have fallen, and this must be so; but they must be perverse indeed who will say, 'This branch, that bough is withered, now there is nought to see.'

In all things, it is the beginning and end that are interesting. The love of men and women – is it only when they meet face to face? To feel sorrow at an unaccomplished meeting, to grieve over empty vows, to spend the long night sleepless and alone, to yearn for distant skies, in a neglected home to think fondly of the past – this is what love is.

Rather than to see the moon shining over a thousand leagues, it sinks deeper into the heart to watch it when at last it appears towards the dawn. It never moves one so much as when seen, pale green over the tops of the cedars on distant hills, in gaps between the trees, or behind the clustering clouds after showers of rain. When it shines bright on the leaves of oak and evergreen, and they look wet, the sight sinks deep into one's being, and one feels, 'Oh! For a friend with a heart', and longs for the capital.

And must we always look on the moon and the blossoms with the eye alone? Nay, in the very thought thereof, in the spring though we do not go abroad, on moonlit nights though we keep our chamber, there is great comfort and delight.

A well-bred man does not show strong likings. His enjoyment appears careless. It is rustic boors who take all pleasures grossly. They squirm and struggle to get under the blossoms, they stare intently, they drink wine, they link verses, and at last they heartlessly break off great branches. They dip their hands and feet in springs; they get down and step on the snow, leaving footmarks; there is nothing they do not regard as their own.

It was a most strange way in which some people of this sort behaved who went to see the Kamo festival. The sights, said they, were very late in coming, and meanwhile it was useless to be on the staging. So they went into an inner room, where they drank wine, ate food, and played checkers, backgammon and other games. They left someone on the staging, and when he cried 'It's coming', they all rushed up pell-mell, fit to burst their livers, and pushing forward the blinds leaned out till on the point of falling. They stared as if they did not mean to miss a single sight, making remarks on everything, and then, when it had gone by, they went down again, saying 'Until the next comes.' It seems that all they wanted was to see the sights. The better sort of people in the capital doze, and see nothing at all. Young people, and those of the lower orders, those serving the shrines, or those in attendance on others, do not stretch forward and look over people's shoulders in an unsightly way, and there is no one who is intent on seeing at all costs.

With the soft beauty of hollyhocks that are just hung everywhere about, the charm of stealthily approaching carriages before the break of day, when you guess, that is so-and-so and that is so-and-so, and there are coachmen and servants you know by sight – it is not wearisome to watch all sorts of folk, some queerly, some gaily dressed, going to and fro.

When night falls, whither have gone the carriages that stood in rows, and the close ranks of people? They soon become scarce, the noise of carriages dies down, blinds and mats are taken away. The scene grows to loneliness before one's eyes, saddening indeed as one feels that this is the way of the world.

To see the streets is to see the festival. You know from the many people you recognize, of the crowd who pass to and fro before the staging, that the number of people in the world is not so very large – so small, indeed, that even were you appointed to die only when all these had passed away, you would have but a little time to wait.

If you pour water into a large vessel, and make a tiny hole in it, though it drips but a little, yet if it goes on steadily leaking, soon there is none left.

Of all the many people in the capital, there cannot be a day when someone does not die. Even if it is only one or two in a day, though there will be days when many will be taken to

Toribeno, to Funaoka, and other moorland places, there is no day on which none are taken.

Therefore the dealers in coffins can never make enough to keep a stock.

Young and strong, it matters not, the unforeseen is death. That you have escaped it until today is a miracle, for which to be thankful. Can you even for a little space think tranquilly of life?

It is like making with backgammon counters the pattern called *mamagodate*. When they are arranged you cannot tell which will be taken; but when you count, and take one, the others seem to have escaped; and yet, when you count again, and light on one after another, not a single one remains.*

When soldiers go forth to war, knowing they are near to death, they forget their homes, they forget their own selves. In a thatched hut, withdrawn from the world, peacefully enjoying the rocks and streams, vain it is to hear of these things and feel that they concern you not. Into the still recesses of the mountains shall not the enemy Change come warring? To face that death is the same as to march to the field of battle.

---

* *Mamagodate.* An arrangement of black and white checkers in the following order.

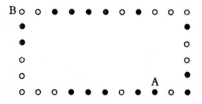

If you count clockwise starting from A, and remove the 10th checker, and continue from the next, then remove the 10th checker therefrom, and so on, all the white checkers but B will be removed. Continuing then from B in the same way, all the black checkers are taken, leaving only B, which, strictly speaking, should also be removed.

138. Once a certain person had all the hollyhocks taken down from his blinds when the Kamo festival was over, saying they were no longer of any use. I thought this was unfeeling, but as it was done by a great man, supposed it was the proper thing. But there is a poem by Lady Suō:

> . . . In vain they hang on the blinds,
> The withered leaves of hollyhocks
> That we cannot see together . . .

which she is said in her *Collected Poems* to have composed about the withered leaves of hollyhocks stuck on the blinds of the main building [of the palace]. In the descriptions of old poems, too, we find 'A poem sent attached to withered hollyhocks'. In the *Pillow Book* also it is written, 'Things that excite regret for the past – withered hollyhocks', which strikes me as very fine and touching. In the *Tales of the Four Seasons* Kamo no Chōmei writes, 'The hollyhocks after the festival remained on the beaded blinds.'

How is it possible to throw away without regret what anyhow of itself anon must wither? Again, since it is said that the medicinal scent bags hung on the curtains in the doorways of the Palace are changed for chrysanthemums on the 9th day of the ninth month, the irises must remain until the chrysanthemum time. After the dowager empress Biwa had passed away, Ben no Menoto composed a stanza on seeing that withered iris medicinal scent bags still hung on the inside of the old curtains.*

---

* Kenkō's cryptic account of the poetic exchange involving Ben no Menoto is omitted by Sansom. It assumes a knowledge of the poems involved. Kenkō writes: 'Ben no Menoto composed the poem: "roots out of season I leave hanging here", and Gō Jijū replied with the one: "Though there are iris leaves".' The full poems depend on much word-play, but might be rendered:

Irises through my tears; their roots out of season I leave hanging here and give voice to my sobbing.

Though there are iris leaves in the scent bags here, I little thought I would see her chamber in such ruin.   (NJP)

139. Trees that it is desirable to have about the house are the pine and the cherry. Of pines the white pine [parvifolia] is good. Single blossoms are best. There used to be double cherries only at the capital at Nara; it is of late they have become common. The blossoms at Yoshino and the Sakon cherry at the palace are all single. The double cherry is exaggerated and specious. It is an oddity. It is better not to plant it. The late cherry too is disagreeable, and those which insects have got at are nasty. Of plums the white and the pink, blooming early, and the double red with its lovely scent, are all charming. The late plum flowers together with the cherry, so that it is less favoured, and sad it is to see its blossoms, overwhelmed by the cherry, clinging withered to their branch.

Fujiwara no Teika said that the single ones, blooming first and falling, gladdened the heart sooner, and so he planted single plum trees near his eaves. Two of these are left to this day at his residence in Kyōgoku, on the side of the house facing south.

Willows again are pleasing. More lovely than all the flowers and red autumn leaves is the young maple of the fourth month. Both orange and vine should be old and big.

Flowering plants are kerria, wisteria, iris and pink. For ponds the lotus. Autumn plants are *ogi* [reeds], *susuki* [eularia], *kichikō* [kikyō], *hagi* [lespedeza], *ominaeshi* [patrinia], *fujibakama* [eupatorium], *shioni* [aster], *waremokō* [burnet], *karukaya* [another patrinia], *rindō* [gentian], *kiku* [chrysanthemum], *kigiku* [yellow chrysanthemum], and *tsuta* [ivy]; *kuzu* [creeper] and *asagao* [convulvulus] are good, on a small, low bank, not in too great profusion.

Apart from these, all uncommon things, with names that sound hard and foreign, and unfamiliar flowers, are not at all desirable. Strange and rare things are mostly what amuse people of bad breeding. It is better to be without such.

140. 'The body dies, the treasure left behind.' Such is not the conduct of a wise man.

It is stupid to store up bad things. It is vain to set your heart on good things – and still more regrettable if they are many and extravagant.

It is an unseemly thing when people quarrel over what is left behind, saying 'I must get it.' If there is someone for whom you intend it afterwards, better surrender it to him while you are alive. Have those things which cannot be dispensed with for your daily use. All other things are better done without.

141. His eminence Gyōren of the Hiden'in, whose lay name was Miura, was a warrior beyond compare.

A man from his old house came to talk to him, and said: 'What the people of Azuma say can be trusted. The people of the capital give fair answers, but they are false.'

The sage answered 'No doubt you think so; but I have lived long in the capital, and now that I have grown used to them, my view is that these people are not worse at heart. It is because in general they are soft-hearted and feeling, that, being unable to refuse plainly what others ask, they cannot speak out fully. They do not answer weakly thinking to deceive, but, as they are all poor people who cannot do as they would, it must often happen that, against their will, they are unable to carry out their intentions. The Azuma people, though I am one of them, have in truth no warmth of heart, and are deficient in kindness. Being altogether strong-minded and outspoken, they say 'No' at the outset and there is an end of it. Being prosperous and rich, people trust them.'

Such was his explanation. This good man's speech was in-elegant and harsh; so that I wondered how he could have any thorough understanding of the sacred teachings; but after this saying, I came to admire him, and felt that it was a good thing that he, out of the many, with such a kindly side, should have charge of the temple.

142. Even men who seem heartless sometimes say a good thing.

A certain wild barbarian of fearful appearance, meeting a neighbour, said, 'Have you any children?' 'Not one,' he replied. 'Then you cannot know the "pity of things", and all your doings must be with an unfeeling heart.' This was a terrible saying, but it must be so, as he said, that by children men come to feel the 'pity of things'. Without the natural affections, how could there be any love and compassion in the heart of such a man. Even those who are without filial affection, when they themselves have a child, realize their parents' love.

One who has forsaken the world is entirely alone and destitute; but it is wrong to despise utterly the common flattery and strong desires of those whose ties are many. If you put yourself in their place you will in truth feel grief. For the sake of their parents, for the sake of wife and child, they will forget shame, and they will steal.

Therefore is it better, rather than only to put bonds on thieves and punish wrongdoing, so to rule the world that the people of the world do not suffer from hunger and cold. When a man has not a common livelihood he has not common feelings. When a man is in extremities he steals. When the world is ill-governed then the pains of cold and hunger are present, and crime will not cease.

Having caused a people to suffer and break the law, then to punish them is a cruel business.

And further, if you ask how to do good to men, the answer is, if those above give up their wasteful luxury, soothe and foster the people, and encourage agriculture, there can be no doubt that those below will profit.

It is he who, having the common share of food and clothing, yet will do evil, that must be called the true thief.

143. When you hear folk talking of the splendid way in which a man has met his end, you would think that they would feel admiration if only it were said that it was peaceful and undisturbed; but foolish people add talk of strange and doubtful appearances, and praise his words and behaviour according to their own likings – which, one feels, is contrary to what he himself would have wished in life.

This great occasion is one which even incarnated saints cannot determine, and scholars of wide learning cannot calculate. If one's own heart is not at fault, it matters not what others see and hear.

145. The bodyguard Hata no Shigemi said to the palace guard and lay-priest of Shimotsuke Shingan, 'You are destined to fall from your horse. You should take great care.' Shingan did not believe it, but one day he fell from his horse and died.

People thought this saying of one so skilled in the art was miraculous. They asked what the sign was. He said 'He had a very loose seat, and was fond of spirited horses. That is why I made the prediction. When have I been mistaken?'

146. Myōun, chief priest of Enryakuji, meeting a diviner asked 'Am I in danger by the weapons of war?' The diviner replied, 'Indeed the sign is there.' 'What is the sign?' he asked. 'Your lordship being one who is not likely to be in danger of a violent death, the mere fact that you should think of it and ask the question is already an omen of that danger.'

And he did actually die struck by an arrow.

147. People have started to say of late that if the burning of herbs on the skin known as *moxa* is applied in too many places, a man becomes unclean for the sacred offices. No such thing can be seen in the precedents or the rites.

148. People over forty, in applying the moxa, have a rising of vapours unless the spot below the head of the tibula is burned. It must be applied here.

149. Rokujō [a powder made from deer horns] should not be put to the nose and smelled. It is said to contain a small insect which enters by the nose and feeds on the brain.

150. It is often said that a man who would acquire any accomplishment should take care not to let others know while he is yet unskilful, for it is by coming forward after having thoroughly studied and learned that he will gain admiration.

Such people, however, cannot acquire a single accomplishment. A man who, from the time he is awkward and untrained, will mix with those who are skilful and not be ashamed of laughter and ridicule, and who stubbornly continues in his attachment, even though without the natural gift, will as the years go on, by dint of persistence and care, at last reach a degree of skill greater that those who, being gifted, are indifferent. His high virtue recognized, he will gain an unequalled name.

Some of the most skilful men in the world have at first been said to be incapable; great shame has been put on others.

But if a man strictly observe the rules of his way, and keep a rein on himself, then no matter what way it be, he will be a scholar of renown and be a teacher of multitudes.

151. A certain person has said, that accomplishments in which skill is not attained by the age of fifty should be abandoned. Their zealous study will bring them to no goal. People cannot laugh at an old man, and for him to mix with the multitude is a pitiful and unpleasant sight.

It is better altogether, and more seemly, to give up all tasks and be at leisure. He is of low understanding who spends a whole life irked by common worldly matters. If there is a thing you feel is desirable, then, though you may have it taught you, it is well to withdraw when once, knowing the substance thereof, you are no longer in darkness. But to withdraw without having had any desire from the first – that is best of all.

152. The sage Jōnen of the temple called Saidaiji was bent at the loins, his eyebrows were white – he had in truth a look of high virtue. When once he came to the imperial precincts, the home minister Saionji crying 'Lo! How venerable!' appeared to feel great faith in him. Lord Suketomo seeing this said, 'It is because he is an old man.' And some time after he came, the tale goes, to the minister, leading a shaggy dog, wondrous old and lean, whose hair had fallen out, and said, 'Is not this a venerable sight?'

153. When the lay-priest and counsellor Kyōgoku Tamekane had been captured and was being led to the Rokuhara surrounded by soldiers, Lord Suketomo near Ichijō saw this and said: 'This is noble. To die thus [for the emperor] ought to be a man's object in living!'

154. It was he who, taking shelter from the rain in the gateway of the Tōji temple where a number of cripples were assembled, and seeing that they were all deformed in various ways, some with arms and legs bent, some twisted, some turned backward, thought to himself, 'They are, every one, singular freaks. By all means, they must be cherished.' But as he gazed at them, soon the feeling

of interest wore off, and he began to find them ugly and loathsome, and thought, 'There is nothing like that which is simple and ordinary.' When he returned home, though hitherto he had been fond of dwarf trees in pots, and used to seek those out that were strangely bent and twisted to rejoice his eyes, he now felt that their charm was gone, that it was like being fond of yonder cripples, so he pulled up and threw away all his trees that were planted in pots. This must have been the case.

155. A man who would follow the world must first of all be a judge of moods, for untimely speeches will offend the ears and hurt the feelings of others, and so fail in their purpose. He has to beware of such occasions.

But falling sick, and bearing children, and dying – these things alone take no account of moods. They do not cease because they are untimely. The shifting change of birth, life, sickness and death, the real great matters, is like the surging flow of a fierce torrent. It delays not for an instant, but straightway pursues its course.

And so, for both priest and layman, there must be no talk of moods in things they must needs accomplish. They must be free from this care and that, they must not let their feet linger.

It does not turn to summer after spring has closed, nor does the fall come when the summer ends. The spring betimes puts on a summer air, already in the summer is the fall abroad, and anon the fall grows cold. In the tenth month comes a brief space of spring weather. Grass grows green, plum blossoms bud. So with the falling of leaves from the trees. It is not that the trees bud once the leaves have fallen, but, because they are budding from beneath, the leaves unable to withstand the strain perforce must fall. An onward-urging influence is at work within, so that stage presses on stage with exceeding haste.

This again is exceeded by the changes of birth, age, sickness and death. The four seasons have still an appointed order. The hour of death waits for no order. Death does not even come from the front. It is ever pressing on from behind. All men know of death, but they do not expect it of a sudden, and it comes upon them unawares. So, though the dry flats extend far out, anon the tide comes and floods the strand.

156. The banquet when a minister takes office is usually held in a suitable place lent for the purpose. The one for the minister of the left from Uji was held in the Tōsanjō Palace. Though it was at the time occupied by the emperor, his Majesty was pleased to move elsewhere as it had been asked for.

Though there is no particular reason for it, it was an ancient practice to borrow the palace of the dowager empress.

157. If we take up a pen, it suggests writing; if we take up a musical instrument, we think of making music. If we take up a wine cup, we think of wine; if we take up dice, it suggests gambling. Ideas always come from association with acts, and we should never even for a moment indulge in wrongful amusements.

If we just glance at a verse of holy writ, without effort we are aware of the text that follows and precedes. So of a sudden the evil of many years may be reformed. If we had never chanced to open the book at that moment, how should we have known this? Such is the virtue of association.

If, without any impulse of the heart whatever, we kneel before the Buddha, take up the bell, take up the book, then even while we are carelessly performing pious tasks, a good work is of itself being done. If even with wandering minds we sit on the prayer mat unawares we become absorbed in contemplation.

Action and principle are fundamentally the same. If the outward appearances do not offend, the inward reality is certain to mature. We should not insist on our unbelief, but honour and respect these things [i.e. religion].

158. A certain person asked, 'What do you understand to be the reason for throwing away what is left at the bottom of a wine cup?' I replied 'One talks of *gyōtō* [bottom congealing], so I suppose it means throwing away what congeals at the bottom.' 'No,' he said, 'that is not so. It is *gyotō* [fish path].* It is to leave something to pour out and rinse the place which the mouth has touched.'

---

* Fish path: because a fish, though swimming in the great waters, is said to keep to one path. So the wine which is left in the cup, when finally thrown away, must flow over the same path as that which was drunk, and thus cleanse the place the lips have touched.

159. The *mina-musubi* is a series of knots tied in a cord, so called because it resembles the shell called *mina*. This is what a certain person of high degree said. It is a mistake to say *nina*.

160. Surely it is wrong to say *utsu* [knock up] instead of *kaku* [hang], of a tablet over a gateway.

Kadenokōji no Nihon Zemmon said *kaku*.

It must also be wrong to say *utsu* of a staging for sight-seeing. It is usual to say *utsu* of planking laid on the ground. Of stagings one should say *kamau* [construct].

Similarly it is wrong to say *goma taku* [burn the sacred fire]. One says *goma suru* [make the sacred fire] or *shū suru* [do the ritual].

In *gyōbō* [practising the dharma] it is wrong to read *bō* as *hō*. It should be read *gyōbō*, said the chief priest of the Seiganji.

There are many similar cases in words we commonly use.

161. The blossoms are said to be in their prime 150 days after the winter solstice, or 7 days after the equinox; but it is on the whole correct to say 75 days from the first of spring.

162. The rector of Henjōji temple for a long time made a habit of feeding the birds in the pond. He spread food about up to just inside the temple, leaving one door open, and then, when a countless number of them had got inside, entered himself, shut the place up, and caught and killed them.

Some children cutting grass heard what seemed to be fearful things going on. They told people about it, and the men from the village rose and entered the temple, where they saw the priest, mixed up with a mass of frightened, fluttering geese, knocking them over and wringing their necks.

They seized him and brought him to the commissioner's court. He was sent to gaol, with the birds he had killed hung round his neck.

This happened in the time when Counsellor Mototoshi was commissioner.

163. The people of the Bureau of Astrology had an argument as to whether there should be a dot in the first character used to write *taishō* [a technical term for the ninth month].

The lay priest Morichika said: 'The Konoe regent has a writing on astrology, with notes on the back in the hand of Yoshihira. There it is written with the dot.'

164. When people meet they are never for a moment silent. They always speak. Listen to what they say, and it is for the most part unprofitable talk – popular rumours, gossip about people, doing little good and great harm to themselves and others. When conversing of such things, they do not know that it is without profit for either of them.

165. It is unpleasant to see how people from the east mix with people of the capital, and people of the capital go to the east to set themselves up in the world, and priests of every sect leave their monasteries and temples – all mixing in a society with customs not their own.

166. When we look at the tastes with which men busy themselves, it is as if, having made a snow buddha on a spring day, they would fashion ornaments of gold and silver and jewels, and erect a shrine and a tower for it. Is it likely that they will be able to get the building ready and install the image safely in its place? So long as men's lives also appear to last, and all the while are melting from beneath like snow, many are the tasks they look forward to complete.

167. It is the usual thing for those who are devoted to a particular art to say, and to feel in their hearts, when they are watching a performance of some other art, 'Ah! If this were only *my* art, I should not thus look on without interest.' But this is quite a wrong feeling. Rather if they be envious of the knowledge they do not possess, should they say 'Alas! How enviable! Why did I never learn this?' To parade one's own wisdom and strive with others is of the same sort as a horned animal lowering his horns, a tusked animal baring his tusks. For man not to boast of goodness, not to strive with others, is virtue.

It is a great error to be superior to others. Those who, being of high estate, or exceeding talent, or famous lineage, feel themselves superior to others, even though they do not say so in words, offend somewhat in their hearts. They must take care to forget these things. It is such pride as this that makes a man appear a fool, makes him abused by others, and invites disaster.

A man who is truly versed in any art will of his own accord be clearly aware of his own deficiency; and therefore, his ambition being never satisfied, he ends by never being proud.

168. When an old man excels in knowledge and skill in one particular thing, so that it is said: 'When he is gone, of whom shall we enquire?' then it is not in vain that he still lives, to uphold the cause of the aged. But though this is so, his very devotion to this one thing means that he has lived his whole life for it alone – which seems stupid.

Let him say, 'I have forgotten now.' Even though he knows thoroughly, if he speaks carelessly and at random, people will ask 'Is he really so talented after all?' And besides, mistakes cannot help occurring. To say 'I cannot tell for certain', is to be thought all the more a true master of his art. More painful still is it to listen, thinking all the time 'It is not true', to what is being told about a subject he does not know, with a boasting air, by one who really ought not even to discuss, however diffidently.

169. It has been said that the term such-and-such a 'ceremony' was not used until the reign of his Majesty Go-Saga, and is a word which has recently come into use; but the lady-in-waiting of Princess Kenrei, who was again at court after Go-Toba's accession, has written that 'there were no changes in the "ceremonies" from former days.'

170. To go without any special object to a person's house is a bad thing. Even if we go on business, as soon as it is over, we should immediately leave. It is very wrong to stay a long time. Sitting there face to face, words are wasted, the body fatigued, the mind disturbed, time is spent to the hindrance of other things, all without profit to either party.

But it is bad, too, to talk as if it were tiresome to us. When the subject is disagreeable to us, we should, on the contrary, say so.

It is a different matter when one after our own heart, who desires our company, is at leisure and says 'Stay a little longer! Today let us have a quiet talk.' Every one has, at times, the 'green eyes of Juan Chi' [eyes that are glad to see someone].

It is a pleasant thing when a person comes without business and leaves after a quiet talk. Joyful, too, to get a letter just asking how you are, after a long silence.

171. People playing at shell-matching [where they seek matching halves among a heap], if they leave alone those in front of them, and look all around elsewhere, behind others' sleeves or under their knees, will find the shells in front of them covered by others while they are searching.

Skilful players do not appear to take theirs from anywhere at random; they only match those close at hand, and yet it is they who match most.

When placing checkers at the edge of a checker-board and flipping them, you do not keep your eye on the checker opposite in order to strike it. It is by looking well at your own end, and by flipping straight along the squares near you that your checker is sure to hit its mark.

In all things, we must not look for favour from without. We must make ourselves right. Duke Ch'ing Hsien's words were: 'Do good, and ask not what lies ahead.'

It must be so, too, in the art of preserving the state. If no care is given within, and the country, lightly and selfishly ruled, is disturbed, then not until distant provinces rebel, as they surely will, is some plan sought to subdue them. It is like what is written in books on medicine, that a man is a fool who, after exposing himself to the wind and lying in the damp, complains to the gods of his sickness. The fact is, people do not know that if they keep straight in the Way, doing kind deeds and relieving the sorrows of others under their eyes, their influence will be far-reaching. Yü marched to subdue the Miao clans, but he did better by withdrawing his army and spreading virtue in the land.

172. When a man is young the blood runs too hot within him. His heart is moved by things, his passions and desires are many. He will risk his life so that it is as easily destroyed as a ball is made to roll. He delights in splendour, and he wastes treasure. Anon, abandoning these, he grows worn and ragged; and as his fiery temper reaches its height, he struggles with circumstance, feels envy and shame, and from day today his desires are unsettled. Deep in venery, ardent with passion, he admires only the example of those who have endangered their bodies that should last a hundred years, and lost their lives in going fearless on their way. He cares not to live out a long life, but dragged whither his desires lead him he becomes the talk of long generations. It is the work of youth to spoil life. The spirit of an old man declines. He grows simple and calm, and is not moved by the senses. His heart is perforce at peace, and he therefore does no useless actions. He takes care of his own person, and is without grief, while anxious that others shall not suffer. The wisdom of the old is as much superior to that of youth as the beauty of the young is superior to that of age.

173. The history of Ono no Komachi is very uncertain. Her decline is described in a book called *Tamazukuri*. There is an opinion that this book was written by Kiyoyuki, but it is entered in the list of the works of Kōbō Daishi [Kūkai]. The Daishi passed away at the beginning of Shōwa [834-48]. Whether Ono was in her prime after that is also doubtful.

174. A dog which is good with a small hawk becomes, they say, bad for a small hawk once it is used with a large one. True it is indeed that to follow great things is to abandon small things.

In all the manifold affairs of men, there is no deeper feeling than delight in the Way. This is the true great thing. Once a man has heard the Way, and inclined his heart towards it, what task will he not abandon, what business will he undertake? Is even a man who is a fool inferior in heart to a clever dog?

175. There are many things in this world that are hard to understand. It is hard to understand why people take pleasure in pressing wine on others the first thing on every occasion, and forcing them to drink against their will. The drinker's face shows great distress; he knits his brows, and seeks a chance to throw away the wine, or to escape unobserved. But they catch him and hold him back, and recklessly make him drink; so that an elegant person suddenly becomes a madman, behaving foolishly, and a healthy person before our very eyes turns into a man with a grave illness, falls and lies unconscious. A stupid way to spend days of rejoicing! Until the morrow, with aching head, and eating nothing, a man lies groaning. As if cut off from life, he does not know what happened yesterday, he neglects important affairs, public and private, and the result is calamity. To treat people like this is to be lacking in kindness as well as to offend against courtesy, while he who meets with such treatment cannot but feel hatred and regret. If such things did not happen among ourselves, and we were told that this was the custom in some foreign country, we should think it strange and incredible.

It is sad, too, in its effect upon others. A person whose thoughtful manner has been looked upon with admiration will lose all reserve, talk a great deal, his cap awry, the cords of his garments loose, his skirts tucked up high, his whole abandoned appearance such that he cannot be recognized as his usual self. Women will openly comb up the hair over their foreheads, without any shame lift up their faces and laugh aloud, grasp the hand of another holding a wine cup, and the worst of them will take food and put it to the mouths of others, or themselves eat in an unseemly way. Men shout at the tops of their voices, each singing and dancing for himself. Old priests are summoned, who bare their black and dirty shoulders, and go through contortions so unsightly that even those who look on with enjoyment are hateful and disgusting. Others, again, ludicrously tell fine tales about themselves, others weep drunken tears, while the lower sort of people, reviling one another and quarrelling, are foolish and terrifying at the same time. The whole thing is disreputable and miserable. They end by seizing forbidden things; they fall off verandahs or from carriages and horses and do themselves hurt. The class that do not ride or drive reel along the streets and scatter unspeakable things up against walls or under gateways. Old priests, wearing their scarves, lean on the shoulders of little children and stagger along, talking nonsense – a pitiful sight.

How is this the sort of behaviour to bring profit in this world or the next?

In this world it brings many calamities. Wealth is lost and sickness gained. Though it is called the Chief of a Hundred Medicines, yet it is from wine indeed that all sicknesses arise. Though it is said that by drinking we forget our sorrows, it is in truth drunken men who call to mind past griefs and weep.

As for the next world, a man loses his understanding; his virtue is consumed as with fire. 'He who takes wine and gives it to another to drink is born for five hundred births without hands' is the teaching of the Buddha.

And yet, although it thus seems that wine is a thing to be shunned, there are occasions when it cannot be dispensed with. On a moonlight night, and a snowy morning, or underneath the blossoms, when we are talking with light hearts, all pleasures are increased if the wine cup is brought forth. When an unexpected friend comes in on an idle day, it is cheering to entertain him with wine. It is exceedingly good to have fruits and wine bestowed on you from within the curtain, in unaccustomed precincts.

Very pleasant in some small place in winter to cook your own meal and sit with a close friend and drink deep. Pleasant again, when stopping somewhere on a journey, on hills or moors, to cast around for food, and sit drinking on the grass. It is very good for one who is much averse to wine to drink a little when pressed. Joyful, also, when a person of high rank is pleased to say 'Take another, that is not enough.' Joyful, too, to become [over the wine] fast friends with a drinker whose company you desire.

Whatever has been said [above], a drinker is amusing, and his faults are forgiven.

A man exhausted with drinking sleeps till late in the morning; and then, when the master of the house opens the shutters, he is confused, and with sleepy looks, his queue in disorder, not stopping to put on his clothes, he gathers them up in his arms, drags them along and flees. Then it is an amusing and proper sight, the back view of him in his shirt tails, showing his lean and hairy shanks!

176. The black door is in the room where the emperor Komatsu, still remembering after his ascent to the throne the old days when as a private person he performed menial tasks himself, used to cook his own food. It is called the black door because it was blackened by smoke from the kindling-wood.

177. Once when the Kamakura shogun Munetaka was giving a game of football, he was in doubt what to do, as the garden had not dried after a fall of rain. Whereupon Sasaki, the lay priest from Oki, presented the shogun with a large quantity of sawdust in a cart, which being spread all over the garden there was no trouble about a muddy ground. People were much impressed by this, thinking it fine that he should have kept it ready in case of need. When someone mentioned this fact, and Yoshida no Chūnagon said, 'Why was there no sand ready?' he felt ashamed. The sawdust which they had thought so fine was vulgar and out of place. It has been the correct thing from olden times for the person who has charge of garden affairs to be provided with dry gravel.

178. When some *samurai* who had seen the sacred dance in the inner chamber of the palace, were describing it, and said that such-and-such a person held the Treasure Sword, and so on, one of the women of the party said quietly, 'When his Majesty proceeds to the Detached Pavilion it is the sword of the Day Palace.'

This was admirable. She was it appears an old attendant in the shrine.

179. The priest Dōgen Shōnin brought back from China a complete set of Buddhist sutras, and enshrined them at a place called Yakeno near Rokuhara.

In particular he expounded the Surangama Sutra, and called the place the Naranda temple after the original in India.

This saint said:

> There is a tradition that Ōe Masufusa held that the main gate of the Naranda temple faced North; but in the *Hsi yü chi* or *Fa-hsien chuan* this does not appear; nor can it be found anywhere. It is not clear what was Ōe's intention in saying this.

'The Hsi-ming temple in China,' he said, 'of course faces North.'

180. The 'Sagichō' is the ceremony of taking the mallets and balls which were used at New Year from the Shingon'in to the Shinsen Garden and there burning them. The words 'the pond of the law fulfilled' which they chant refer to the pond in the Shinsen Garden.

181. A learned person said: 'In the words [of the nursery rhyme] "*fure, fure, koyuki, Tamba no koyuki*" [fall, fall, flour-snow, flour-snow from Tamba], the *koyuki* [flour-snow] comes from the likeness of snow to rice flour which is being sifted. "*Tamba no koyuki*" is a mistake for "*tamare koyuki*" [pile up, snow!] and at the end should be sung "*kaki ya ki no mata ni*" [on fences and the forks of trees].' Has this been said since olden times? In the diary of Sanuki no Suke it is stated that the emperor Toba said it when he was a child.

182. The Shijō counsellor Takachika hearing someone say, when a dish called *kara-zake* [dried salmon] had been provided for the imperial table, that such strange things ought not to be supplied, said: 'That might be so if it were wrong to serve his Majesty with fresh salmon; but as that is not so, what objection can there be to dried raw salmon? Is not his Majesty served with dried brook-trout?'

183. We cut off the horns of a bull that gores people, and clip the ears of a horse that bites, as a sign thereof. To let people get hurt through not attaching some sign is a crime in the owner. A dog that bites should not be kept. All these are offences forbidden by the law.

184. The mother of the regent Tokiyori, governor of Sagami, was called Matsushita Zenni. Once, when Tokiyori had been asked to her house, she herself set about cutting round with a small knife and repairing some torn and blackened paper windows [*shōji*]. Her elder brother, Jō-no-suke Yoshikage, who was engaged in preparations for the day, said 'Let me have it. I will give it to such and such a man. He understands these things.' But she replied, 'His work will not be any better than mine,' and

went on pasting square after square. Yoshikage said, 'It would be far easier to repaper the whole window, and besides, the patches look ugly.' But the dame said, 'I mean to do the whole thing altogether later on; but today I am purposely doing it like this. I wish to set an example to young people, so that they may learn that things should be mended only where broken, and so used.'

These were very fine words. The foundation of government is economy. Though she was a woman, what she said was in accordance with the teaching of the sages. Indeed, she was no ordinary person, inasmuch as she had as her son one who preserved the State!

185. Yasumori, commandant of Akita castle and governor of Mutsu, was unequalled as a horseman. When a horse was being led out for him, and he saw that it jumped quickly over the door-sill [of the stable] with its legs together, he would say, 'This is a spirited horse', and have his saddle changed to another. Again, when a horse in stepping forward kicked up against the sill, he would say, 'This horse is dull, and therefore an accident might happen', and would not mount it.

People who knew nothing about the art of riding would not think there was so much to fear.

186. A horseman named Yoshida said: 'Every horse is to be feared. One must know that a man cannot compete with a horse in strength. When about to ride, first of all one should look at the horse carefully, and mark its strong and weak points. Then one should see whether there is anything wrong with bit, saddle and trappings, and if there is anything one does not feel safe about, that horse should not be taken. It is not forgetting to take these precautions which makes a true horseman.' This is the secret of riding, he said.

187. Those who make a business of any art or trade, even if they are unskilful, are always superior when compared with skilful persons who are amateurs. The reason for this is the difference between never relaxing one's care and being always earnest in the one case, and being entirely one's own master in

the other. Nor is this confined to arts and accomplishments alone. In all our deeds and thoughts, to be unskilful but earnest is the source of success; to be clever but wilful is the source of failure.

188. A certain man decided to make his son a priest, and said to him 'You must study, and learn the principles of the faith, and by preaching and so on make this your means of livelihood.' The son did as he was told. First of all, in order to become a preacher, he learned to ride a horse. This was because he thought that it would be regrettable for a priest, who owned neither palanquin nor carriage, when he should be invited to take a service, and a horse sent to fetch him, to fall off because he had a loose seat. Then, because he might be pressed to take wine and food after some sacred rites, and his host would think him dull if he were utterly without accomplishments, he learned to sing [the popular ditties called] *haya-uta*. Having at length begun to be proficient in these two arts, he felt anxious to do better still, and while he was devoting himself thereto, he grew to old age without having had time to learn to expound the scriptures.

Nor is this priest the only one. This thing happens to all people. While they are young they look many years ahead, and are always meaning to study, to exhaust all forms of accomplishments, to carry out great undertakings, and in every way to rise in the world. But all the while they take life easily, they continue in idleness, and pass their days and months troubling to do only the pressing tasks beneath their eyes; and so they grow old having accomplished nothing. They end by never growing skilful in anything, without having gained the position they had thought. Since the years cannot be brought back again, they go on declining, as a wheel runs downhill.

Therefore we should weigh in our minds which is the most important of all the things which we would desire to make our aim in life, and having decided which is the first thing, we should abandon all others and devote ourselves to that one thing.

When in the space of a day, nay, even of an hour, a number of tasks present themselves, we should perform that one of them which is even by a little the most profitable, and neglect all others in order to hasten on the important matter.

If we are loth to abandon any, and take up all, then not even one thing is accomplished.

It is like, for example, a man playing checkers, who without wasting a single move, outstrips his opponent by throwing away little to gain much. For it is an easy matter to leave alone three checkers and attack ten, but hard to leave ten and attack eleven. Though he ought to attack the number which is largest even by one, when the others mount up to as many as ten he feels reluctant, and it is hard to change to checkers that are very little more numerous. The desire to take this and not to throw away that is the way to lose that and not to gain this.

A man living in Kyōto has urgent business at the East Hill, and though he has already arrived there, it occurs to him that it would be of greater profit to go to the West Hill. Then he should turn back at the gate, and go to the West Hill. He thinks: 'I have come so far, I might as well do this business. As I did not fix a day, I will go to the West Hill some other time after I get back.'

Thus a moment's laziness becomes the laziness of a whole life — a thing to be dreaded.

If you are determined to do a certain thing, you must not grieve at the failure of other things, nor be ashamed at the scorn of other people. Without giving up everything for it, the one great thing cannot be accomplished.

Among a large number of people, one said, 'They say *masuho no susuki*, *masoho no susuki*, and so on. The Sage of Watanabe has had the explanation of the difference between these types of *susuki* [pampas grass] handed down to him.' The priest Tōren, who was present, heard this. It was raining at the time, and he said, 'Have you a rain-coat and an umbrella? Lend me them. I am going to call at the sage's house to learn about these *susuki*.' They said 'Do not be so hasty. Wait till the rain stops.' To which he replied, 'What a wrong thing to say! Does a man's life wait till the rain, clears? If I should die, or the sage pass away, could I ask him? Then he ran out, and going thither, learned. This is the tradition, a rare and admirable tale, it seems to me.

In the book called *The Analects* it is written 'To do things speedily brings success.' Even as he felt in doubt about the *susuki*, so should we feel about the truths of the great matter.

189. Today you mean to do a certain thing, but some urgent affair you had not foreseen arises, and you spend the whole day thereon. Or again, the person you await is hindered, and someone comes whom you did not expect. You fail to do what you had hoped, and succeed only in something you had not intended. The thing that was troublesome passes off without difficulty, the thing that should have been easy causes great anxiety. The daily happenings are quite other than you had thought; so with the passing of a year; and so, likewise, with the course of a whole life. You may think that everything will go contrary to your hopes, and yet sometimes all of its own accord falls out as you desire. Nothing in fact is certain. That all is uncertainty − this, being truth, is the only thing in which we cannot be mistaken.

190. A wife is a thing a man ought not to have. I like to hear a man say, 'I am still living alone', and so on. To hear it said, 'So-and-so is getting married' or 'He has taken such-and-such a wife, and they are now living together', lowers him extremely in my estimation. For one thinks poorly of a man who marries a quite ordinary person because, forsooth, he has made up his mind she is a fine woman; while, if she is a handsome woman, and he cares for and cherishes her as if she were his own image of Buddha, then one wonders how he can go so far. More regrettable still is it in the case of a woman who manages the work of the household; and grievous when children come, and she nurses and loves them. When she becomes a nun after her husband's death, and grows old, her condition is mean though he is no longer alive.

Living day in, day out with a woman, of whatever sort she may be, she must lose her attraction and become disliked. The woman, too, must grow indifferent. It is by keeping apart, and going to stay with her from time to time, that an intimacy is reached that even the passing of months and years will not destroy.

It is a pleasant change then to go and stay from time to time.

191. I think it a pity to hear a man say that things do not look their best at night. Indeed it is only at night that brilliance and colour are pleasing. By day let your appearance be simple and sober, but at night it is well to wear bright and gay garments.

Good-looking people look even better at night by lamplight; and it is pleasant to hear the voices of people talking guardedly in the dark. Perfumes and music, too, are most pleasing at night-time.

It is good to see someone coming late to the palace, on a night when there is nothing much afoot, carefully attired. Young folk make no distinctions, but are always observant of one another, so that it is desirable, in particular just at those times when ceremony is dispensed with, to dress carefully, without reference to the occasion.

It is pleasant to see a handsome man who has been to the bath, or a woman who, when night comes, has withdrawn [from her mistress' presence] and taken her mirror and made up her face and so on.

192. To shrines and temples too, on days when there is no festival, it is better to go and worship by night.

193. When an ignorant man thinks to judge another, and know the measure of his wisdom, he is quite sure to be wrong.

It is a great mistake for a foolish man, who is quick and skilful only at the game of checkers, and sees that a wise man is poor at that game, to come to the conclusion that the other's wisdom does not equal his own, or for any expert in one of the various accomplishments, seeing that others are ignorant thereof, to think himself their superior. If priests who read the scriptures and priests who practise meditation each, in their mutual judgments, think the others not equal to themselves, then they are both wrong.

A wise man sees others with unerring eyes,

194. Suppose, for example, that a man makes up a false tale in order to test others. Some are simple, and will take it to be true, and may be judged according to what they say. Some will be too credulous, and imagine an even worse falsehood, which they will add thereto. Some, again, will think nothing of it and pay it no heed. Some, again, will think it a trifle doubtful, and will turn it over in their minds, while neither believing nor disbelieving. Some, though they do not think it likely to be true, confine

themselves to saying 'Quite so', because it is what another has told them. Others, again, make all sorts of guesses, and pretend to understand, and nod and smile with a wise air, though all the while they know nothing whatever. Some will surmise [that they are being tried], and think 'Ah! That's it!' but will still be suspicious, for fear of mistakes. Some will clap their hands and laugh, thinking there is nothing unusual. Others, again, though they understand, do not say that they know, but without commenting on its unlikelihood, let the falsehood pass in the same way as one who does not know the truth.

Some at once understand the purpose of the falsehood, and without the least deceit will fall in with the intention of its maker, and lend him their aid.

Even when stupid people are jesting among themselves, before one who *knows*, these various characteristics are plain to him, without any chance of concealment, from their speech and their faces. The better then can an enlightened man see us deluded ones, even as one looking at a thing in the palm of his hand!

But one must not liken to tests of this sort the expedient devices used to teach the doctrines of Buddhism.

195. As a certain person passed along the Kuga Nawate [a path running between rice-fields], someone wearing [the silk upper and lower garments known as] *kosode* and *ōguchi* was carefully washing a wooden image of Jizō which he had placed in the water in a rice-field.

While he watched, unable to understand, two or three men in *kariginu* [court dress] appeared, and saying 'Ah! Here he is', accompanied the man away.

It was the Naidaijin of Kuga – who at ordinary times was a man of great parts and lofty character.

196. When the sacred car of the Tōdaiji [used to transport the deity Hachiman] was being taken back from the lesser shrine of the Tōji in Kyōto to be reinstalled in Nara, some nobles of the Minamoto clan went with it. Lord Kuga, who was then a general, was clearing the way ahead, when the prime minister of Emperor Tsuchi asked, 'How about clearing the way around the shrine?

Ought this to be done?' He answered only, 'It is the business of military families to know how an escort should act.'

Later he explained thus. 'The prime minister has read the *Hokuzanshō*, but did not know the opinion expressed in *Saikyū*. The fact is, it is in particular at shrines that the way should be cleared, for fear of all the familiar evil spirits and deities.'

197. The term *jōgaku* [fixed complement] is not only applied to priests in the various temples. The *jōgaku* of women servants at court is also mentioned in the *Engishiki* records of ceremonial. It is the general term for any fixed number of public servants.

198. The term *yōmei* [signifying a nominal post] is not confined to *yōmei no suke* [a nominal provincial official of the second rank]. There is also a *yōmei no sakan* [that is, a nominal provincial official of the fourth rank]. This is written in the work on administration called *Seiji Yōryaku*.

199. The priest Gyōsen of Yokawa said: 'China is a country of *ryo*; they have not the sound *ritsu*. Japan, being a country of *ritsu* only, has not the sound *ryo*.*

200. The bamboo called *kuretake* has narrow leaves; the *kawatake*, broad leaves. That near the gutter in the palace is *kawatake*, and that near the Jijū Pavilion is *kuretake*.

201. Of the *stūpas* called *taibon no sotoba* and *gejō no sotoba*, the *gejō* is at the bottom and the *taibon* up the hillside.

202. There is no book or written authority for saying that the tenth month is the month-without-gods, and should be avoided for the sacred rites. Perhaps it is only because there happen to be no festivals at the various shrines during this month that it has the name.

Some hold that in this month all the gods assemble at the great

---

* Musical scales were divided into two types: *ryo* and *ritsu*.

shrine of Ise, but there is no authority for this. If such were the case, it in particular would be made a festival month at Ise; but there is no instance of this. There are many instances of an imperial progress to the various shrines in the tenth month. For the most part, however, they have been unlucky.

203. There is nobody left nowadays who knows the procedure of hanging up a quiver at the house of one who has been degraded by the emperor.

When the sovereign suffers from sickness, and in general in times of trouble among the people, a quiver is hung up at the Tenjin shrine at Gojō. The deity called *Yugi* at Kurama also had a quiver hung up for him.

When the quiver borne by a police official was hung up outside a house, people could not enter or leave it. Since this custom died out, it has become the practice nowadays to place a seal [on the gate].

204. When criminals are flogged with rods, they have to be placed on a frame, and bound thereto. It is said that nowadays there is nobody who understands the shape of this instrument, or the proper method of attachment.

205. What is called the 'dedication oath' of the high priest at Mt Hiei was first written by the Abbot Jie.

The term 'written oath' is not known to students of the law. In the holy reigns of the past government was never carried on by means of written oaths, which have become common in recent times. Nor do the laws hold that there is defilement in fire and water, but only in the vessels that contain them.

206. Once while the minister of the right Tokudaiji, at the time he was chief magistrate, was holding a council of the magistracy at the middle gate, the ox of the official Akikane got loose, and climbed up on to the daïs, where it lay down and chewed the cud. Everybody said that this was a grave portent, and the ox should be sent to the diviners. The minister's father, the prime minister, however, said: 'An ox cannot make distinctions. Since

he has legs, he will climb anywhere. A wretched official, coming once in a way to duty at the palace, could not catch his miserable ox!' He returned the ox to its master, and changed the mats where it had lain; and nothing evil happened.

'When we see some wonder,' he said, 'and do not wonder at it, then the wonder is destroyed.'

207. When they were levelling the ground for building the Kameyama palace, there was a great mound where innumerable large snakes were clustered together. They made a report to the emperor, saying these were the gods of this place. His Majesty asked what ought to be done, and they all said that as the snakes had occupied the ground since olden times, it was out of the question to dig them up and throw them away.

This minister alone said: 'What evil can be worked by such creatures in imperial ground, when an imperial palace is to be built! The gods are not malevolent. They will not be offended. All we have to do is to dig them up and throw them all away.'

So they broke up the mound, and threw them into the Ōi river, and there was no evil consequence whatever.

208. In tying up the strings of a scroll of prayers, the usual thing is to cross them, and then make a loop which is thrust sideways under and between the two crossed parts. The chief priest Kōshun of the Kegon'in, untied one done in this way and did it over again, saying: 'This is a new fashion, and very ugly. The neatest way is to roll the strings round and round, and then pass a loop under them from top to bottom.'

He was an old man and so knew about this sort of thing.

209. A man who had a dispute about a rice-field, and lost his case, out of spite sent people to reap that field and bring in the crop. First they reaped and carried off the crop from the fields on the way, and when someone said, 'What is the meaning of this? These fields were not in dispute', the reapers replied, 'There is no reason for reaping these fields, but as we have come out to do a wrong thing anyhow, it doesn't matter where we reap!' This was a most curious argument!

210. The bird called the *yobukodori* is merely known as a spring bird, and it is nowhere written exactly what sort of a bird it is.

In certain writings of the Shingon sect there is given the procedure for performing the invocation of spirits, at the time when the *yobukodori* sings. This is the bird called the *nue*. In one of the *Manyōshū* long poems it is mentioned in connection with the rising mists and the long days of spring. The descriptions of the *yobukodori* and the *nue* seem to agree.

211. In nothing at all should we put our trust. It is because foolish people are deeply trustful that they know hatred and anger.

Though you have power, do not trust in it. The strong perish anon. Though your treasures are many, do not trust in them. They are easily lost in a moment of time. Though you have talent, do not trust in it. Confucius himself was unsuited to his times. Though you have virtue, do not trust in it. Even Yen Hui was unfortunate. Do not either trust in the favour of princes. The death penalty comes quickly. Because you have servants in your train, do not trust in them. They may rebel and run away. Do not trust either in the feelings of others. They will surely change. Do not trust in promises. Truth is rare.

If you put trust neither in yourself nor others, you will rejoice when good comes, and when evil comes you will not grieve.

If there is width to right and left, there is no obstruction. If there is distance before and behind there is no confinement. In narrow spaces things are crushed and shattered.

When the mind is narrow and severe, we come into collision with things, and are broken in the conflict. When the mind is broad and gentle, not a hair is harmed.

Man is of the spirit of the universe. The universe is without limits. How shall the nature of man differ therefrom? When it is great and open and infinite, joy and anger do not touch it, nor does it suffer at the hand of circumstance.

212. The autumn moon is of loveliness without end. Nobody is more pitiable than a man who cannot see the difference, and thinks the moon is the same at all times.

213. When putting fire in the brazier before his Majesty, tongs
are not used. It has to be transferred straight from an earthenware vessel, so that in piling up the charcoal care must be taken
lest any fall out.

At the imperial progress to Yahata one of those in attendance,
wearing white vestments, put on charcoal with his hands; whereupon a certain learned person said: 'There is no objection to
using tongs on days when white clothes are worn.'

214. The music called *Sōfuren* [feeling love for a man] is not so
called from a woman's love of a man. It was originally 'The
Premier's Lotus', and the characters have been changed. It is
music in praise of the lotuses, of which he was very fond, that the
minister Wang Chien of the kingdom of Chin planted in his
garden. From that time he was called the lotus statesman.

Similarly the piece called *Kaikotsu* should be written with
different characters to those used at present. This is because there
was a country of terrible savages called the country of Kaikotsu.
These savages were subdued by the people of Han, and when
they afterwards came to Han they performed the music of their
own country.

215. The court noble Taira no Nobutoki, telling tales of the past
in his old age, used to relate how the lay priest Saimyōji, formerly
the Hōjō regent Tokiyori, once sent for him in the evening, and
he said he would go at once. His ceremonial dress was missing,
and while he was doing one thing and another, a second message
came, saying 'Is it that you have no dress of ceremony? If so,
being night-time, it does not matter what you wear, but come
quickly.' So he put on a crumpled robe, and went in his indoor
clothes. When he arrived his host brought out a wine-vessel and
earthenware wine-cups, saying 'I asked for you because it would
be lonely drinking this wine alone. There is no food to eat with
it. All the people in the house will have gone to bed, but please
go and see if you can find something suitable anywhere you like.'
So he took a taper, and searched in every corner till, on a shelf in
the kitchen, he found a small earthenware bowl with a little bean
sauce at the bottom. He went back and said 'I have found this.'

The lay priest said 'That will do', and in good humour drank several cups of wine and grew merry.

'In those days,' said Nobutoki, 'it was like that.'

216. The lay priest Saimyōji, when on a pilgrimage to Tsurugaoka, took the opportunity of visiting the lay priest Ashikaga, chief of the horses of the left, after first sending a messenger to announce himself.

The feast prepared was this: the first dish, dried abalone; the second, prawns; and the third, rice cake; and that was all. There were present the master of the house and his wife, and the abbot Ryūben sitting on the side of the host.

When Tokiyori said, 'I fear you will not have any of those dyed cloths of Ashikaga which you present to me every year', he replied, 'I have some ready.' And they brought out various dyed cloths, which Saimyoji had made up into garments by women in his presence, and afterwards gave to the lay priest Ashikaga.

This story was told by people who saw it at the time, and were living until recently.

217. A certain rich and prosperous man said: 'A man should give up everything and devote himself to gain. If he is poor, it is not worth while living. If he is not rich he is not a man. If you would acquire wealth, what you must do is this: first you must cultivate the proper frame of mind, and that is none other than to dwell in the conviction that life is everlasting, and never for a moment to regard its impermanence. This must be your first care. Next, you must satisfy not a single one of your wants. In this world, the desires of men, for themselves and others, are without end. If you give way to your lusts, and think to satisfy your desires, then even a million pieces of money will not last for a little while. Desire never ceases, but there comes a time when treasure is exhausted.

With treasure that has a limit, you cannot satisfy desires that are without end.

If desires begin to grow in your heart, beware; be firmly on your guard, thinking an evil thought has come to destroy you, and do not fulfil your smallest want.

Next, if you treat money as a slave, and look on it as a thing for your use and service, then you will never escape from poverty.

Do not subdue it to your uses, but fear it and reverence it, like a master, like a god.

Next, you must feel neither anger nor hatred even in the face of shame. Next, you must be honest, and firmly keep your covenants.

To a man who seeks profit by heeding these rules, riches will come just as fire attacks that which is dry, as water flows downwards.

When money accumulates unceasingly, then the heart is happy and peaceful, though you take no thought of feasting and drinking and women and song, though your home is unadorned and your desires unfulfilled.'

This was what he said. Now, in order to fulfil their desires, men seek wealth. The reason they regard money as wealth is that by its means they can satisfy their wants. If a man has desires but cannot satisfy them, or has money but does not use it, he is exactly the same as a poor man. Where can he find happiness? I understand these rules to mean that we should cast away our mortal hopes, and not be grieved by poverty. Rather than to seek happiness by satisfying our desires, it is far better to be without wealth. For a man who suffers from boils, rather than to find pleasure in washing them, it would be better not to suffer from them at all. When it comes to this point, there is no difference between poverty and wealth. The ideal is the same as the actual, and avarice is like unselfishness.

221. Even now old officials in the magistracy still relate how it was the usual thing at the Kamo festival, in the periods of Kenji [1275-78] and Kōan [1278-88], to see, as the emblems carried by the bearers, a horse made of four or five rolls of curious blue cloth, with rushes for tail and mane. This they wore attached to their clothes, which were of a spider-web pattern, and went along singing the burden of some song; and people felt that it was done to amuse them, and were satisfied.

But of late the emblems have become more unusually extravagant year by year. All sorts of heavy things are worn in great numbers, both their sleeves are held up by others, and they are not even able to hold a spear themselves. It is an unpleasant sight to see them, distressed and panting for breath.

[222, 223 and 224 are omitted, being unintelligible in translation]

225. Ō no Hisasuke says that the lay priest Michinori selected certain dances that were amusing, and taught a woman named Ise no Zenji to dance them. She wore a white robe, with a sword, and an *eboshi* [court cap], and thus they were called *otoko-mai*, men's dances.

Zenji's daughter, who was called Shizuka, followed her in this profession. This is the origin of the female entertainters called *shirabyōshi*.

They sang the stories of gods and buddhas. Later Minamoto no Mitsuyuki composed a great number of others, and there are also some that are the work of the emperor Go-Toba, which his Majesty was pleased to teach to the dancer Kamegiku.

226. Yukinaga, ex-Governor of Shinano, who was famed as a scholar in the time of his Majesty Go-Toba, once, when called upon to take part in the debate in the Bureau of Music, forgot two of the virtues mentioned in Po Chü-i's poem *Dances of the Seven Virtues*, and so was nicknamed the 'youth of five virtues'. He took this so much to heart that he threw up study, and fled the world. The priest Jichin, who had compassion for anyone able to do something, even down to the lowest, and took them into his service, assisted this lay priest of Shinano.

This Yukinaga wrote the *Heike Monogatari* and taught a blind priest named Seibutsu to recite it.

His writing about the Hiei temples is particularly good, and he wrote with an intimate knowledge about Yoshitsune. He leaves out a great deal concerning his elder brother Noriyori, perhaps because he did not know much about him. With regard to soldiers and fighting, Seibutsu, being an easterner, asked questions of soldiers, and Yukinaga wrote down what he told him.

The present *biwa* priests [itinerant entertainers who recite the *Heike Monogatari* to the accompaniment of the lute (*biwa*)] have imitated the natural voice of this Seibutsu.

227. The *Rokuji Raisan* is a collection of prayers made by a disciple of the saint Hōnen named Anraku, which he used to recite. Later a priest called Zenkambō of Uzumasa fixed the notes and the pitch, and put it in the form of a chant. This was the beginning of the *ichinen no nembutsu* [the doctrine that a single heartfelt recitation of the name of the Buddha Amida was sufficient to win salvation]. It commenced in the time of the emperor Saga.

The *Hōji san* was likewise originated by Zenkambō.

228. The *Shaka Nembutsu* of Sembon [the recitation of the name of Sakyamuni] was begun by the saint Nyorin about the Bun'ei period [1264-75].

229. They say that a good carver of images always uses a slightly blunt knife. The knife of Myōkan did not cut at all easily.

230. In the Gojō Palace there was a ghost. Counsellor Fujiwara relates that while some of the courtiers were playing checkers in the room with the black door, someone lifted the blind and looked in. They looked round to see who it was, and there was a fox, in the shape of a man, peering into the room. 'It's a fox!', they shouted, whereat it fled, bewildered by the noise.

A very inexperienced fox, and a failure as a ghost!

231. The lay priest Sono no Bettō was without equal as a cook. Once at a certain person's house a splendid carp was produced, and everybody there thought they would like to see the lay priest prepare it, but hesitated to ask him, because they felt it might be wrong lightly to make such a proposal. The lay priest, however – being that sort of person – said 'Just now I am preparing a carp every day for a hundred days, and I must not miss today, so that I am very anxious to undertake this one.' He then cut up the carp.

Everyone was much interested, thinking it very fine and proper, said somebody who told the story to the lay priest, the Kitayama prime minister; whereupon he replied, 'This sort of thing disgusts me. It would have been better if he had said "I should like to be allowed to prepare this, if there is no one else to do it." How could he possibly be preparing carp for a hundred days?'

The person who told me this said he found it admirable. It was indeed very admirable.

It is always better to be simple and uninteresting than to be interesting but affected.

In entertaining strangers, though it is well enough to try to make things interesting, it is better still just to produce them in an ordinary way.

When making gifts, too, it is true kindness to say 'I should like to offer you this', and to add no embellishment.

232. All men should be without wisdom and without talent.

A certain person's son, who was in appearance and otherwise not unpleasing, in his father's presence wished to join the talk, and so he made quotations from the classics. It sounded clever enough, but one wished he had not done so in the presence of people who deserved respect.

Again, at a certain person's house, they wanted to hear a blind minstrel sing, and a lute was sent for. One of the bridges was missing, so he ordered one to be made and fixed. A guest – a well-looking man – asked if they had the handle of an old wooden dipper, and looking at him, I saw that his nails had been let grow. He played the lute himself! Now there is no need to go to such trouble for a blind priest's lute, and it disgusted me to think that he was making himself out an expert in the art.

Someone said that the handle of a dipper, being what is called 'bent-wood', was unsuitable.

The smallest things about young people are noticed, good or bad as the case may be.

233. If you wish to be free from all blame there is no better course than to be always sincere, to make no distinctions of person, but treat everyone with respect, and to be sparing of words.

Though men and women, young and old, should all be like this, it is particularly true of young and good-looking people that those of pleasant address are always remembered.

All blame from others is due to pretending experience, making oneself out to be skilful, putting on superior airs, and looking down on people.

234. It is a great mistake, when someone asks you a question, to give a perplexing answer because you think he surely must know, and it seems foolish to state the facts just as they are. He may know, and yet have asked in order to make sure; and besides, why should there not be some person who really does not know? It would be more sensible, and sound better, to tell him plainly what he asks.

It is a careless thing, when writing a letter to someone about something you know yourself but he has not yet heard, merely to say that so-and-so has done a foolish thing, for you will get a letter back asking what happened.

Since it occurs that some people miss hearing the most widespread tales, what is there wrong in writing and telling him so as not to leave him in doubt?

It is inexperienced people who do this sort of thing.

235. An evil-doer never walks just as he please into a house that is occupied. But into an empty house wayfarers enter at will, and foxes, owls and suchlike things there take up their abode as if the place belonged to them, because there is no human presence to withhold them; and even such strange shapes as goblins and so on appear.

In mirrors, too, because they have neither colour nor form, all sorts of reflections come and show themselves. If a mirror had colour and form there would be nothing reflected. It is emptiness that best contains things.

So when momentary thoughts wilfully enter our hearts, it must be because we really have no heart. If the heart has a master, the heart will not be invaded by innumerable things.

236. In Tamba there is a place called Izumo. They brought thither the worship of the Great Shrine, and set up a beautiful building. A man by the name of Shida, who was in charge of the district, invited one day in the autumn the venerable Shōkai and many others. 'Come,' he said, 'and let me offer you some rice

cake in honour of Izumo', and then led them thither. They all worshipped, and were filled with great faith. The stone dogs before the shrine stood, contrary to custom, facing backwards. Shōkai was much impressed by this, crying, 'O, how fine! Now there must be some very deep reason for this.' He wept with admiration, and said, 'Sirs, did you not notice this excellent thing? That was bad of you.' They were all surprised, for in truth there was nothing of the sort elsewhere, and they said they would carry home the tale to the capital. The holy man, growing more and more enthusiastic, called an elderly priest, with an intelligent face, and said, 'There must surely be some reason for the position of the dogs before your shrine. I wonder, Sir, if you could tell me what it is.

'Yes,' he replied, 'it is a trick some mischievous children have played.' And approaching the dogs, he put them straight and went on his way.

The holy man's tears of admiration were all for nothing.

237. Should things be placed on a stand made of strips of willow-wood lengthwise or crosswise, according to what they are?

Things like scrolls should be placed lengthwise, and tied with twisted paper passed through the space between the wood.

Sanjō, the minister of the left, said it is a good thing to place ink stones lengthwise, as the pens do not roll off.

The calligraphists of the Kadenokōji family never for a moment put them lengthwise, but always made a point of placing them crosswise.

238. Chikatomo, of the imperial bodyguard, set down in writing seven articles which he called 'Self-Praise'. They are all trifling things, about horsemanship.

Following this example, I have these seven causes for self-praise.

i   Once I was walking in company with a number of people looking at the blossoms. Near the Saishōkō-in I saw a man galloping a horse, and I said, 'If he gallops that horse again, the horse will fall and he will tumble off. Watch a moment!' We

stood and looked, and he galloped the horse again. When h
came to a stop, the rider pulled the horse down, and rolle
into the mud.

They were all much impressed by the truth of my words.

ii When the present emperor was still crown prince, and h
residence the palace at Madenokōji, I happened once to go o
business to the apartment of the Horikawa counsellor, wh
was in attendance on his Highness. He had spread out befor
him the fourth, fifth and sixth volumes of *The Analects*, an
said, 'Just now the prince wished to see the passage abo
purple and vermilion, and he looked in his book but cou
not find it. He told me to look more carefully and I am no
searching for it.'

I said, 'It is at such and such a place in the ninth volume.'

'Ah! I am glad,' said his Lordship, and took the volum
with him.

Now such a thing as this is quite ordinary, even for a chil
but people in olden times used to praise themselves for th
smallest things. Once when the cloistered emperor Go-Tob
asked Fujiwara no Teika whether it was wrong, in one of th
Imperial poems, to use the words *tamoto* and *sode* in the sam
verse, he replied 'Why should it matter? There is the poem:

> Aki no no no
> Kusa no *tamoto* ka
> Hana susuki –
> Ho ni idete maneku
> *Sode* to miyuran.'

Even this has been set down in writing, and a great fu
made, such things being said as, 'It was divine grace, and gre
good fortune for the art of poetry, that he should have had th
original poem in his mind at the right moment.'

The Kujō prime minister Koremichi, too, in his petition
the throne for promotion, set down all manner of trivi
articles in praise of himself.

iii The inscription on the bell of the Jozaikō-in was composed b
Lord Arikane. Yukifusa Ason wrote it out in a fair hand, ar

was going to get the bell founders to copy it, but the lay-priest in charge brought out the draft and showed it to me, and there was written the verse:

> Hana no hoka ni
> Yūbe wo okureba
> Koe hyakuri ni kikoyu*

As it appeared to be derived from a Chinese rhymed verse with lines ending in *yō* or *tō*, I said 'Is not *hyakuri* a mistake?' Whereupon he said 'It was a good thing that I showed it to you. This will bring me great credit.' So he sent a message to the writer, and it turned out that it was a mistake. The answer came, 'It should be *sū-kō* [a long way].

iv Once I went with a large party on a pilgrimage to the Three Pagodas. Inside the Jōgyō Hall of Yokawa there was an old tablet, with the inscription 'Ryōge-in'.

One of the priests said very importantly, 'Tradition says that it has never been settled whether this is the work of Sari or Kōzei.'

'If it is Kōzei,' I said, 'it should be signed on the back. If Sari, there would be nothing written at the back.'

The back was thick with dust, and foul with insects' nests. After it was dusted and wiped, we all looked carefully and there saw quite plainly the names of Kōzei, his rank, and the date – whereat everyone was highly interested.

v In the Naranda temple the holy Dōgen was preaching, when he forgot which were the Eight Disasters, and, upon his asking if anybody remembered, none of his disciples knew them; when I, from the congregation, said, 'Are they not such-and-such?' and made a great impression.

vi I once went with the archbishop Kenjo to see [at the palace] the incantation by perfumes, and he left before the end. He could not see his bishop anywhere outside the room, so he

---

* If you spend the evening far beyond where the flowers bloom, its note will be heard a hundred leagues away.

sent back some priests to look for him, who were a long time
because, they said, it was impossible to find him in a great
crowd of persons who all looked alike. 'How tiresome!' he
said, and asked me to find him. So I went back into the room,
and soon brought him out with me!

vii On a bright night, of the 15th day of the second moon, I
went to worship late at the temple of Sembon. I entered from
the back, and alone, with my face well hidden, was listening
to the service. A beautiful woman, of figure and style beyond
the ordinary, pushed her way in and sat so close as to press on
my knee, and the perfume of her garments was all but
communicated to me. I felt this inopportune and moved
away, when she edged up and did the same again. I then left.

Afterwards, an old lady in the service of a high personage,
said to me in the course of a gossip, 'I once despised you very
much, as a person cold beyond measure; and there is someone
who feels quite angry with you for being unfeeling.' I said, 'I
do not understand you at all', and the matter stopped there.

Later I heard about this, and it appears that on the night of
that service someone had recognized me from her private
apartment [in the temple] and had had the idea to dress up one
of her waiting women and send her out, saying 'If he gets a
chance he will speak to you. Go, and tell me what happens. It
will be amusing.'

239. On the 15th day of the eighth month, and the 13th of the
ninth month, the constellation is *Lou* [Aries]. This is a very bright
and clear constellation, so that these are good nights for enjoying
the moon.

240. Warm is the love of a man who will visit his mistress
undeterred by prying eyes and watchful guardians, and many a
thing happens, anon to be looked back to feelingly and never
forgotten.

It must make a man feel very small just to take to himself a wife
because she is approved by his parents and brothers.

And when some lonely woman says she will go 'whither the
stream takes her', and will marry anyone if he is prosperous, even

an ugly old priest or some strange man from the provinces – and the middleman makes out each party to be desirable – what an unlovely thing for a man thus to take a wife he knows not and to whom he is unknown! And whatever can they talk about, when they meet?

If they could speak together of all their months and years of suffering, and the hard road they have travelled, there would be no end to their talk; but when others have made arrangements for them, it must be very stupid and disagreeable.

Even if the woman is beautiful, a man of low birth, getting on in years, and ill-favoured, will think, 'Alas! that she should waste herself on such a wretched person as me.' She will go down in his estimation, and he will feel ashamed to face her. This is a very unhappy state of things.

A man who does not like to picture himself standing beneath the clouded moon on a night when the plum blossom smells sweet, or brushing at daybreak through the dewy moor – such a man had better have nothing to do with women at all.

241. The full moon does not keep its roundness even for a while. It quickly wanes. To those who give no heed it may seem that in a single night there is no great change. So with the growth of sickness. It stops not for a space, and the moment of death is already near. While sickness is not yet severe, and he is not approaching death, a man feels that life will always go on in the same way, and thinks first to complete a number of worldly tasks and then to devote himself to religion. Meanwhile sickness comes, and he is at the gates of death, without having accomplished one of his desires. Vainly he regrets the wasted months and years, and vows that if this time he gets better and his life is saved, he will not cease to labour night and day to complete this task and that. But anon he sinks, and deranged, beside himself, he passes away.

Such is what always happens. Let people, then, quickly take this thing to heart.

If a man thinks to turn to the Way in the leisure left after he has fulfilled his desires, his desires will never come to an end. What can a man do, in this life that is like a dream? All desires are wicked thoughts. If desires enter your heart, you should recognize that wrongful impulses are leading you astray, and should not do a single thing. If you forthwith abandon all, and turn to the Way, then you are free from hindrance and trouble, and the mind and body are at lasting peace.

242. That we are forever the servants of our likes and dislikes is entirely for the sake of pleasure and pain.

Pleasure is liking and loving. We never for a moment cease to seek it. Of the causes of our pleasure and our desires, first of all comes fame: fame is of two sorts – praise of conduct, and of talent. Second is fleshly lust, and third is appetite. Of all our desires, none can match these three.

This is a perverted view of life, and from it arise innumerable disasters. It is better far to seek none of these.

243. When I was eight years old I asked my father, 'What is a Buddha?' My father said, 'A Buddha is what a man grows into.' I asked again, 'How does a man become a Buddha?' My father again answered, 'He becomes one by the teaching of a Buddha.' Again I asked, 'Who taught the Buddha who teaches him?' He answered again, 'He also became a Buddha by the teaching of a Buddha before him.' Once more I asked. 'And what sort of a Buddha was that very first Buddha who began to teach?' When I said this my father laughed and said, 'I suppose he fell from the sky or sprang up from the earth!' He was so hard pressed with questions that he could not answer, but he used to tell the story to everyone with great delight.

COSIMO CLASSICS

COSIMO is an innovative publisher of books and publications that inspire, inform and engage readers worldwide. Our titles are drawn from a range of subjects including health, business, philosophy, history, science and sacred texts. We specialize in using print-on-demand technology (POD), making it possible to publish books for both general and specialized audiences and to keep books in print indefinitely. With POD technology new titles can reach their audiences faster and more efficiently than with traditional publishing.

> **Permanent Availability:** Our books & publications never go out-of-print.

> **Global Availability:** Our books are always available online at popular retailers and can be ordered from your favorite local bookstore.

COSIMO CLASSICS brings to life unique, rare, out-of-print classics representing subjects as diverse as *Alternative Health, Business and Economics, Eastern Philosophy, Personal Growth, Mythology, Philosophy, Sacred Texts, Science, Spirituality* and much more!

COSIMO-on-DEMAND publishes your books, publications and reports. If you are an Author, part of an Organization, or a Benefactor with a publishing project and would like to bring books back into print, publish new books fast and effectively, would like your publications, books, training guides, and conference reports to be made available to your members and wider audiences around the world, we can assist you with your publishing needs.

Visit our website at www.cosimobooks.com to learn more about Cosimo, browse our catalog, take part in surveys or campaigns, and sign-up for our newsletter.

And if you wish please drop us a line at info@cosimobooks.com. We look forward to hearing from you.

Printed in the United States
60164LVS00001B/63